"Men are bro
process. Ofte.
perpetuated by a wrong model of manhood. *No Wimps* speaks to the flawed models of manhood that may have been used to identify and call forth manhood. It offers thoughtful answers to help every man repair his thinking and embrace a biblical model of manhood. It is a must read for men and their mentors guiding them into 'real' manhood."

Tom Lane

Apostolic Sr. Pastor, Gateway Church,
Southlake, TX

"Extremely entertaining and thought-provoking. *No Wimps or Weaklings Allowed* will help many understand the difference between toughness and strength. God's anointing is all over the pages of this book. I would wholeheartedly recommend it to any man."

Pastor Warren Samuels

Founder, Next Worldwide Missions
and President, H2H

"Great and heroic feats are usually the result of many *strong men* quietly accepting their responsibility to stand their place on the wall! Strong men face these battles of identity internally and continuously for the sake of those they love. Thank you, David, for giving us a tool for waging this war against a false, confusing narrative of what it means to be a 'gospel-centered-man' in these confusing times."

Tony Elenburg
Recording Artist and President, RioVida Music

"In today's climate, the world needs to see what a man of true strength looks like. In *No Wimps or Weaklings Allowed,* David Vestal debunks stereotypical images of manhood and helps us see how real men are designed to live and act. This is a must-read for everyone."

Jonathan Shibley
President, Global Advance

"Much of the brokenness in our society is due to men not having a true understanding of biblical manhood. *No Wimps or Weaklings Allowed* will cause you to think deeply about your own journey through manhood as well as encourage those you may be fathering or mentoring in manhood. You will be challenged and encouraged by David's style of writing and his life experiences."

Tim Chapman
President, Cross Generational Ministries

"I remember when David, my dad, sat me down to talk about manhood before I left for college. At the time, I didn't know how important that conversation was. The misrepresentation of masculinity that young men today are facing is a *big* issue. *No Wimps* describes how men wrongly view themselves and act out of that missed self-identification. It's a must-read for men of all ages."

Michael Vestal
Senior Project Engineer
TZA Labor Management Solutions

"It is clear that, biblically, the man is to be the head of the family. There is a feeling that men must be tough. David Vestal is a man of integrity who has a great perspective on what a man of God should look like."

Paul Pogue
President , Minuteman Disaster Response
Ministry Builders

NO WIMPS OR WEAKLINGS ALLOWED

HOW TOUGH GUYS BECOME STRONG MEN

DAVID VESTAL

DANALYN PUBLISHING

For more information, visit DavidVestal.com.

Edited by Blake Atwood of BA Writing Solutions LLC: BlakeAtwood.com

ISBN 978-0-578-48747-2

Dedicated to my grandfather,
Johnny Vestal

He taught me more about being a man than anyone I have ever met. He didn't do it with words but with example.

When God gave me the idea for this book, he said to me, "David, the more you die, the more your family lives." I have thought of those words throughout the pages of this manuscript.

Just as Jesus laid down his life for his bride, I watched my grandfather lay down his life for *his* bride (my grandmother) so that she could live. Pop showed me what true, sacrificial love looks like day in and day out. Consequently, I learned how to lay down my life so my bride can live to be whom she is called to be.

Pop was a small man in stature but a giant in my eyes. He demonstrated a strength that very few men have. I wanted that strength.

Pop, I thank you for your sacrificial demonstration to me and all the Vestal family. Your words of kindness and wisdom did not fall on deaf ears. Your demonstration of a strong man did not go unnoticed by me. Thank you for being a man.

Warrior

A warrior has a Plan.
A Worriar doesnt wait
Till the fight comes.
In the midst of the Battle if
your not prepared, your going
to Lose the Battle. You
as a warrior, you prepare
for what battle your going to Face.
Being a Warrior of God, Be prepared
Because if you are in Christ
It requires faith and Action

CONTENTS

ACKNOWLEDGMENTS

Over three decades, God has given me a true example of great strength.

Thank you to my wife, Dana, for being that constant example of God's unwavering love, grace, encouragement, and strength. You have loved me and stood by my side when I was working on my tough side in the trenches of the Dallas Police Department. You have been my biggest cheerleader during this book and the transformation that God continues to bring me through. What a privilege it is to be your husband.

Thank you to my children, Carisa, Caitlyn, and Michael, for loving me through my imperfections and giving me the privilege to be called your dad.

Thank you to the many spiritual brothers and fathers God has brought into my life over the years to demonstrate what a man of God looks like.

I love you all.

INTRODUCTION

"You know, David, the more you die, the more your family lives."

I heard that in my spirit on a regular afternoon drive home from my office. My response was less awestruck and more, well, confused.

"Uh, what's that, God? I have to die so my family lives? What's the precedent for that? Are you sure that's you talking, God?"

I knew it was him, but I chose doubt because I didn't want to have to act upon what he'd just revealed to me. I'd been a Christian for a long time and knew that Jesus was the bridegroom who had willingly given up his life for his bride, the church. I also knew that, as a husband myself, I was supposed to love my wife like Jesus loved the church (Ephesians 5:25).

Which meant just what God had told me during that drive: the more you die, the more your family lives.

So my family could live, I had to die. There's a reason I keep repeating that phrase. God had to repeat it to me multiple times before it finally got through my thick, tough-guy cranium. I didn't want to admit to its truth because I knew dying would be uncomfortable.

Of course, I'm not talking about physical death, but rather putting to death the deeds of your insecurity, self-ishness, and control. Willfully choosing to lay down your preferences, your ego, and your stature—especially if you've always been a me-first tough guy—will make you very uncomfortable.

Jesus always loves sacrificially, meaning it costs something.

Get Comfortable Being Uncomfortable

If I haven't been to the gym in a long time, I dread going back. I know that every part of my body will hurt after that first day back. I'm supremely uncomfortable, and nothing within me wants to go back to the gym the next day because I know it'll hurt even more.

With the men I counsel, I always tell them to get comfortable being uncomfortable. When you truly decide to die so that your family will live, God will take you serious. Consequently, you'll begin to see just how selfish you really are! Every time you turn around, you'll bump into yourself. Selfishness will shine bright. Sacrifice is uncomfortable.

My men get frustrated by this and start complaining: "Is this what life is really all about? Is this going to be my life—being miserable for ever and never really living?" (This is still the tough guy talking.)

The problem with their honest questions is that they're mistaking the beginning of the process for its end. Dying is never the end! What we must look forward to is resurrection *after* death. That's what transforms a tough guy into a strong man.

Jesus was resurrected after his death, and when he rose he had a new body and even new abilities to walk through walls and transcend time and space. He *flew* away when he said goodbye. While you won't receive such superhero tradeoffs when you die to self, you *will* be transformed and begin walking with new power and confidence for the better if you allow your tough guy exterior to die. But you have to truly die to self on a daily basis in order to experience the kind of superhuman strength I'll be discussing for the duration of this book.

Choosing to die to self is the most transforming tradeoff I've ever made, but it's a decision I have to make on a daily basis—just like going to the gym. My muscles are screaming at me to stop after the first, second, third and fourth day, but if I stay the course and get comfortable with being uncomfortable, my muscles will eventually stop hurting and begin growing stronger. They'll start to operate the way they were designed to operate. In time, I'll even become energized by my workouts to the point that if I miss a workout, I'll feel lousy. The habit becomes such an integral part of my life that I can't do without it. The process literally begins to produce life-altering energy that transforms my daily existence.

When I made the decision to start dying to myself and putting my bride first, it was extremely uncomfortable. I didn't want to keep going. It was killing me on the inside. Would I receive anything from my sacrifices or was I going to be miserable for the rest of my life? My thoughts sounded just like the men I counseled. (Even this is obviously all about me.)

Then something strange happened. I began to look forward to serving my wife and my children. Suddenly, it was as if I were operating on a totally different level. Then I began to receive energy and life from putting them first.

I started living as a strong man of God, as the man he'd always intended me to be. In such a life, there's no room for a tough guy. That's why he has to die.

Over the course of this book, you're going to meet nine kinds of tough guys that may all make their home in your heart from time to time. Your job, should you choose to accept it, is to identify what tough guy you still need to wrestle, then let Jesus show you how to fight that man to the death.

3 Differences Between
God's Voice and the Voice in Your Head

1. GOD'S VOICE NEVER CONTRADICTS SCRIPTURE

Holy SPIRIT will NEVER CONTRADICT HIM SELF

SINCE WE KNOW the HOLY SPIRIT INSPIRED SCRIPTURE WHAT he says to us personally will NEVER contradict what HE HAS said in the written word of God.

John 16:13 WHEN the spirit of truth comes, HE WILL GUIDE YOU INTO All the Truth, For HE Will not SPEAK on His own Authority, But WHATEVER HE HEARS HE WILL SPEAK And HE will DECLARE to you the things that are to come.

John 17:17 Sanctify them in the Truth: YOUR Word is Truth.

2. Gods VOICE IS NEVER WRONG

Deuteronomy 18:21-22 you may say to yourselves: How CAN WE KNOW when A MESSAGE HAS NOT BEEN spoken By the LORD?

3. YOUR VOICE SERVES YOU BUT GOD'S VOICE SERVES God

Gods voice is Always God centered And the voice in our heads is MAN centered. THE VOICE in our head will SERVE you. We are wanting to hear Your desire will be to do what God wants if we

Galatians 5:16-17 So I say, walk by the Spirit, And you
will not gratify the Desires of the flesh. For the flesh
Desires what is contrary to the Spirit And the
Spirit what is contrary to the flesh. They are
In conflict with each other, So that you are not
to Do WHATEVER YOU WANT.

ONE

THE TOUGH GUY

I don't know why Johnny hated me, but it surely must have been hate that drove him to chase me seemingly every day for at least a year when I was nine years old.

My saving grace? Equal parts speed and fear. I could outrun the lumbering eleven-year-old bully.

But I couldn't outrun a dead-end.

On that fateful day decades ago, I had nowhere to go. Johnny had trapped me in an alley three blocks from my home. A crowd quickly circled. I wheeled around to face Johnny. I spoke as fast as I could in a vain effort to thwart his advance. If only I could stall him, maybe I could figure out how to get to my house.

are in the Spirit.

But Johnny just kept walking, wordlessly, fearlessly, and wholly intent on one outcome: pummeling me. He had me dead-to-rights—until, out of nowhere, my dad showed up. Apparently, when she saw my predicament, a girl who didn't want to see me die had immediately bolted for my parents' house.

My dad didn't even get out of his blue Chevy pickup. He just cocked his head and said, "David, get in the truck."

I smiled at my feet and my good fortune. I sprinted past Johnny untouched and leaped into the passenger side.

Then Dad said, "You too, Johnny. Get in the back."

I looked at my dad, thinking him delusional. *Wait, what? Didn't you see what almost just happened? That guy was gonna kill me. You want your son dead? What is your problem, Old Man?*

Of course, I didn't say these things out loud or my dad *would* have killed me. But in the minute that it took him to drive us around the corner and to our house, I was fairly certain my dad had lost his mind. He might as well have been driving me to my own funeral.

The crowd that had gathered to witness my sure annihilation followed us. Dad pulled into our driveway and ordered us all into the backyard. The swelling audience jockeyed for best line-of-sight positions over the fence railings.

Then Dad said, "Settle this now, son, once and for all."

So I did.

I don't remember much of that fight, but I know I did pretty well.

Johnny never bothered me again.

What It Means to Be A Man

When I fought Johnny, I'm sure my anger at being picked on all the time had bubbled to the surface. But I'm also sure that my anger boiled over by how infuriated I was with my dad for making me fight, especially in front of the whole neighborhood.

However, when I fought I felt the power of what it means to be a man—at least what I thought it meant to be a man. I can't remember if I was actually declared the winner, but I did hold my own against an older, bigger kid. I remember my dad looking at me as if I'd done a good job.

I didn't know it then, but that fight would set the tone for my life for decades. I was a tough guy because I'd always been the tough guy. When it came to what I thought a man was, winning fights summed it all up pretty well.

Soon after that memorable incident, apparently impressed with my skills, my dad literally started *paying* me to beat up other kids in the neighborhood he thought were stealing from him. As evidence of how this truly and directly affected my future, decades later, the City of Dallas started paying me to take down more bad guys as a Dallas Police Officer in the West Dallas Projects.

I've always known what it means to be tough. I've been shot at, beat up, spit on, cursed out, run over, and stabbed. I've been in the emergency room more times than I can count. I learned to settle my problems with my gun, my fists, or my machismo.

I was a tough guy, for sure, but was I a strong man?

I've always wanted to be the best man I could be—the best husband and the best father. But, as I matured, I discovered that being strong wasn't always the same as being tough. In fact, I don't believe most men really know the difference.

Most of us were raised to be tough, but we have a greater calling to be strong.

The Basis of a Tough Guy

While the rest of this book will dive into the many ways that guys act tough, one issue sits at the heart of every tough man. Whether you want to admit it or not, it doesn't change the truth. It's fear.

Until I was forty years old, I believed I had to fight all my own battles. That day in the backyard with Johnny, I felt abandoned and alone. I'm not sure if that was my dad's intention, but from that point on I felt like I had to fight my own battles. Why? Because I feared letting others control me, feared not being known as a tough guy, and feared letting others get so close that they would see my fears.

I believed that verbal and physical forcefulness settled disagreements. I believed that the tougher I was, the more respect I received. Mind you, I had this mindset *prior* to joining the Dallas Police Department, but ten years on the force certainly accentuated my egotistical leanings.

When recalling my time serving Dallas in a notably crime-ridden area, it seems as if no night passed without some kind of physical confrontation. Some fights I *had* to win because my life depended on the outcome. Other fights I felt I had to win because my pride depended on it. For me, it wasn't enough just to survive another night on duty; I wanted to thrive, to be noticed, to be promoted, and to be congratulated for my toughness.

My commanding officers might as well have been my dad still giving me a few dollars to kick around the neighborhood's petty thieves.

I didn't lose many fights when I was on the force, and I sure didn't lose any arguments. I'm a big guy who knows how to get loud. To get my point across, I can appear threatening on command. I exuded toughness in everything I did.

Of course, this tough-guy act wasn't such an issue on the job, but I couldn't turn the switch off. Who I was while yelling at criminals gradually became too much of who I was as a husband and father. I learned that I couldn't win fights in my marriage by intimidating my wife. I learned that trying to make my children fear me by yelling at them wasn't going to work either. I discovered that leading from a place of fear and intimidation, as I did on the streets of Dallas for all of my working hours, didn't translate to the rest of my life as a leader.

I knew something had to change, but I didn't know that a man had any other options than to portray toughness.

After all, that's what my dad had taught me.

If I couldn't be the "tough guy," who was I?

The Strongest Man I Know

I'm not a fan of professional wrestling. Maybe it's a little too real for me.

But every so often, I'll land on a match while I'm channel-surfing. Even though it seems they've been telling the same basic "story" for decades, I can't help but watch. The characters and venues may be different, but what unfolds holds steady to a compelling narrative that seems never to get old.

Good Guy is getting the snot beat out of him by Bad Guy. Literally, mucus and sweat are flying off of Good Guy's face. Bad Guy pile drives Good Guy for the fifth time, and Good Guy's legs twitch as he lays otherwise motionless at the center of the ring. Bad Guy hops to his corner, arms raised in celebration, with one hand cupped to his ear as if he can't hear the boos resounding throughout the crowd.

The ref starts counting to ten, and, just as he's about to finish, Good Guy drags himself to the side of the mat and tags his partner.

Now the "fight" gets interesting.

Better Guy jumps into the ring. He's younger, faster, stronger, and bigger than Good Guy. Better Guy flexes his chest. The crowd goes wild.

Bad Guy turns around and laughs. He shakes his head and sets his hands as if he's praying. Mockingly, he says, "Have mercy on me." Then he smiles as widely as he can.

Better Guy runs toward Bad Guy.

Bad Guy runs toward Better Guy.

As they both leap into the air feet first, Better Guy's legs extend two inches farther than Bad Guy's. Bad Guy falls to the ground, the wind knocked out of his ego. Better Guy lifts Bad Guy over his shoulders and spins him around like a helicopter. Better Guy throws Bad guy to the ground and quickly falls on top of him.

The ref counts to ten. The match is won. The crowd cheers.

Without fail, this is the most replayed "story" of wrestling.

I've always wondered why Good Guy would even go into the ring when he has Better Guy on his side. Why not just grab a bag of popcorn, sit back, and let Better Guy handle the whole fight? I guess the fight would be over too soon and people wouldn't enjoy it as much as they do, watching Good Guy get the snot beat out of him first. I'm glad that's not me.

Or is it?

The reason why I think this made-up story is too real is that *I* played the part of Good Guy for far too long. Most of us men do, too. But, unlike these staged-for-TV fights, there's a reason us Good Guys always seem to get beat by the Bad Guys.

Because we want to be the toughest guy. We long to be the Better Guy. We want to be the hero, to save the day, to right the wrong, to defeat evil and injustice in all its forms—even if it's wearing a wrestling mask.

But you and I will *never* be the Better Guy. We may be as tough, but we're certainly not as strong.

Yet, thankfully, Better Guy is on *our side* of the ring. We just need to be smarter about when to call him in. Heck, we need to be smarter about calling him in *at all*.

For instance, if I'm always the first guy to go into the ring and get my brains repeatedly kicked in, but I know I have a partner who can defeat Bad Guy with just one move, *why in the world wouldn't I just let Better Guy go first?*

This is a Christian book, so you know where I'm going with this: Jesus is the Better Guy—the Ultimate Warrior.

He always was, always is, and always will be. Yet for so long I lived my life believing I knew better than him. I thought my toughness allowed me to tackle life on my own terms. I believed I could handle whatever life would throw my way. I thought I was mostly good and just needed Jesus when things got *really* ugly. I'd never tag out voluntarily—that's for the weak.

In other words, I believed the lie that Jesus was only to be called on when I was face down on the mat and out of options.

If you're tired of trying to be tough all the time, join me in learning what it means to be strong. Once you see how Jesus paves the way for men to be real men of strength and character and begin challenging yourself to believe, think, and act differently, I guarantee that you will tap into a new level of strength you will never regret. I bet it's what you're longing for this minute.

The first step is the hardest.

Now, Let's Get Real

Most men learn to be tough long before we learn to be strong. We are taught to stuff our feelings, hide our pain, shake it off, put some dirt on it, and get right back up. So, we get pretty good at hiding our emotions.

But there is an immediate insecurity that comes with that method.

"Will they see me hurting? Will they find out that I am not really as tough as I should be? I guess it's up to me to make it happen."

Each of us must discover the true strength we have in Christ. Let toughness die and let the Strong Man live. He is our strength and he is our victory.

Now, take some time to answer the questions on the following pages.

What areas in your life were you challenged to be the tough guy growing up?

We had a neighborhood bully. He was our age. He might have actually been two years older. Looking back we never had in our corner. He wanted to be a part of the neighborhood group of kids. But always putting us down, especially me. Three of the boys in our group played baseball together, one of their fathers was the coach. I couldn't catch, I definitely couldn't bat. One day the bully picked on me in front of all on how couldn't catch. With out warning he threw the ball as hard as he could, I open fits caught the ball. It was like I hit the winning hit of the game I was stunned as to what had happened. My fellow friends were cheering and taunting the bully. There was one other major incident where I fought him and was beating him. I know this because it happened in his front yard. His Dad had to have been watching. He came out and stopped it when his son was loosing. His Dad yelled at me to leave. Pent up rage came out, This guy was always taunting us.

Sports - my parents wanted me be better, meet new people through sports. I hated everything it wasn't my parents who convinced me, it was some coach trying to get me to understand my potential, I wouldn't tell them no.

Being a husband - we want to be there for our spouse
They want us to be the Knight

Being a father: Strong Protector

What areas are you still believing that the fight is all yours?

It's hard to do it God's way

It Requires us to really trust in him

Stop Doubting. Doubting equals fear, stress and creates bad decisions. I'm in physical pain all the time. Walking and setting is like the feeling of running a ten mile run and you hadn't trained for. With head aches. Going through this I have been the most blessed man, And looking back **He** had been preparing me for this moment. I was baptized about four years Back. Everything that has happened was to move me for ward towards are true purpe in Life.

But when others a Round you have doubt, you will Do things you know your Not suppose to be doing you will say things you should never say Because fear is let in, fear says don't be weak or stupid your not doing enough for your situation. Pull your self up, don't be some one else's problem. You should have been better prepared in your Life, what were you thinking.

I know the fight is not mine, deep down inside I know But when I get distracted i Caught off guard. I'm not quick to the Lord. I'm simply reacting to the fear that was created, when it was no different than before or After. The Lord has me and I remember I have him Like a child walking with its mother in a crowd and it Lets go Just grab the hand he will guide you

What areas in your life do you still see the insecurity of being a tough guy? How can you replace those areas with God's strength?

My experiance - its the same when
I get up in fear. It was no different
Jan 8th 2018 or Jan 8th 2020. If he is my Lord
and Savior, and I believe that. It's his will not
Mine. Everyday I catch my self questioning
My self. Is there something I should be doing
for my situation.

With my Wife she wants the traditional
Man. Opens the door, waits on her. who talks
to her, comforts her and keep up with her.
I not that man a lot of the time with the pain.
It's almost as If you don't say it, you won't be it.
So when asked If I would Like to do something
with her, I say simply No. Or I'm asked
to do something Like go hikking a few miles
and I roll my eyes and say no.
Because I'm suppose to be Strong Man.

TOUGH GUY FOCUS VERSES

Exodus 14:13–14: "And Moses said to the people, 'Do not be afraid. Stand still, and see the salvation of the Lord, which He will accomplish for you today. For the Egyptians whom you see today, you shall see again no more forever. The Lord will fight for you, and you shall hold your peace.'"

Exodus 15:3–6: "The Lord is a man of war; The Lord is His name. Pharaoh's chariots and his army He has cast into the sea; His chosen captains also are drowned in the Red Sea. The depths have covered them; They sank to the bottom like a stone. 'Your right hand, O Lord, has become glorious in power; Your right hand, O Lord, has dashed the enemy in pieces.'"

Did any one have something incredable happen to them since last Wednesday?
Did any one hear God?

TWO

THE FIXER

For years, I thought handcuffs and hardheadedness could fix everything.

When I worked as a uniformed patrol officer in the rough streets of the West Dallas Projects, 60 percent of the calls we answered were related to family violence. When a call came in concerning a domestic dispute, we'd arrive on scene and have up to ten minutes to figure out what was going on and devise a solution to fix the problem. Because of our department's strict, no-tolerance policy on family violence, if either party failed to comply after a few minutes, the handcuffs came out and off we went to jail.

Consequently, I learned how to take care of these problems quickly. We had to. After all, we had more calls than we had officers to answer them. When I was on the scene of a domestic situation, you either did what I said or you left in handcuffs.

My fix. Your choice.

But I made a terrible mistake: I applied my domestic violence problem-solving ways to my own family issues.

If I came home from work and my wife was having an issue with any of our kids (or me), I'd assess the situation in five to ten minutes and quickly come up with the right solution—at least the right solution to me.

If somebody didn't like it, out came the handcuffs and somebody was going to jail.

Wait.

That won't work.

And I think it's illegal.

Realizing that my authority at work didn't exactly translate to the same kind of authority at home, I discovered that I couldn't just break out my handcuffs and contain my own domestic issues. I couldn't fix what I saw as problems within my home as easily as I could on patrol. This realization frustrated me to no end, so I'd resort to what I'd always fallen back on before: I became the tough guy. I raised my voice. I pounded my fists on a table or into a wall. I used my size, strength, and considerable loudness to intimidate everyone else into submission.

Need I remind you that this occurred in front of and toward my wife and children?

I imagine they saw more of that nine-year-old fighting in a backyard than the man they needed. I was a grown man throwing temper tantrums assuming that such fits would get me what I wanted: peace and recognition.

In trying to fix the problem, I made it ten times worse. Instead of helping my family, I just got everyone to cower before my tough-guy facade. I'd like to blame my dad, my training, and my job for how I would often shamefully respond to problems in my household, but true strong men don't blame.

They take responsibility.

Control Is Key

Tough guys feel the need to be in control—always. As soon as one iota of control slips from his grasp, the tough guy feels as if his world might fall apart. As long as the tough guy is in control, he can dictate whom he lets into his world. You aren't even allowed in his world unless you agree to his rules.

He has a deep, unhealthy mandate to control his surroundings so that he can maintain his false appearance as the ultimate answer—the prime Fixer—of everything in his universe. He *needs* to be seen as the king at the top of the castle, so he tends to treat everyone else as lower subjects that are to be under his control and in agreement with his philosophies while always looking up to him.

The mind-set of control is laughably egotistical and unrealistic. We control so very little of our lives. Just one tragic phone call is all a man needs to truly understand what little he actually controls. But still we strive to control as much as we can, and we often do that through vain attempts to fix others. If we can fix them, then we can control them. They are in our debt. Tough guys like having people indebted to them. It gives them a feeling of superiority.

They typically won't do things for others without a selfish hook in their actions. They do favors so people owe them. They play the hero so others lift them up. They are somewhat incapable of living for anything else other than themselves.

The strong man lives and operates from a place of security. He doesn't need to control because he doesn't have a need for power. He doesn't need people to be indebted to him because he is comfortable in what he already has. This place of security allows him to live beyond himself. He can help and serve others out of who he already is versus who or what he thinks he needs to be.

A Fabled Son of a God

God speaks to me through movies, and one of my favorites in recent years was *Thor*. As the mythical, hammer-wielding God of Thunder, Thor is next in line to be king of Asgard. But, as Thor's father Odin is crowning him to be the next king, they're attacked by the fearsome Frost Giants. The Asgardians defend their palace, but Thor believes his father should show tough-guy force and retaliate, showing the enemy who's in charge.

Odin's hesitation to act causes an arrogant Thor to fly to the land of the Frost Giants. Thor then takes matters into his own hands. He becomes an epic, retaliating Fixer. He kills hundreds of Frost Giants until his father shows up and prevents him from killing hundreds more. Odin apologizes for his son's behavior, and Odin and Thor return to Asgard.

Once home, Odin tells Thor, "I was a fool to think you were ready. . . . You have betrayed the express command of your king. Through your arrogance and stupidity, you've opened these peaceful realms and innocent lives to the horror and desolation of war! You are unworthy of these realms; you're unworthy of your title; you're unworthy of the loved ones you have betrayed! I now take from you your power! In the name of my father and his father before, I, Odin All-Father, cast you out!"

In other words, the throne needs a strong man, not just a tough guy. Thor's toughness does not put him by his father's side. In fact, it pushes him away.

Thor is cast out to Earth *without* his hammer or his power, but his arrogance is still fully functional. Believing that he could still right the wrongs he's caused and fix the problem, Thor searches for his lost hammer. However, he soon realizes he can no longer rely on the power he once took for granted. He no longer possesses the character to pick up the hammer. He must change how he lives. He's humbled and accepts the consequences of his actions.

However, Thor's brother Loki has been scheming to take Odin's throne and sends a fire-breathing machine called the Destroyer to Earth to kill Thor. As Thor vainly but valiantly fights the Destroyer in an attempt to save earth, he realizes the solution to this problem—and the solution is one he would never have discovered as his former powerful self.

To save the Earth, he must sacrifice himself.

The selfish ambition of the tough guy has been replaced with the selfless humility of a strong man. Thor asks the Destroyer to take his life but spare the earth. The Destroyer complies. With one swipe of his mighty arm, the Destroyer decimates Thor.

But the actions of a strong man are always greater and more life-giving than those of a tough guy.

From his throne in heaven, Odin witnesses his son's sacrifice. With full authority and power to do so, Odin resurrects his son. Thor's hammer flies to his outstretched arm. He receives his power back through his humble actions, then uses that power to defeat the Destroyer and save the Earth.

The Original Son of God

The similarities to Jesus's story are apparent—Frost Giants and fire-breathing machines notwithstanding.

At the appointed time, God's Son left his heavenly

home for Earth. He assumed human form. He shed the throne of God for a manger of man. Although he wasn't banished by his father and his father wasn't displeased with him, such a change of address still had to be shocking. As Jesus grew, he grew into a strong man, full of his Father's love and power.

Because the enemy had come near the dawn of time and threatened humanity, Jesus eventually and ultimately performed the most selfless act in history. For you, for us, for all, he willingly laid down his life. He allowed the enemy to strike him down and kill him.

But from his throne in heaven, Jesus's father witnessed his son's sacrifice. With full authority and power to do so, God the Father resurrected his son. He restored his power and authority over all, which Jesus then used to defeat the enemy and save humanity. *Though he was God, he did not think of equality with God, as something to cling to. Instead, he gave up his divine privileges he took the humble position of a slave and was born as a human being. When he appeared in human form, he humbled himself in obedience to God and died a criminal's death on a cross. Therefore, God elevated him to the place of highest honor and gave him the name above all other names, that the name of Jesus every knee should bow, in heaven and on earth. And under the earth, and every tongue declare that Jesus Christ is Lord, to the glory of God the Father.*

Paul says it better in Philippians 2:6–11:

Being in very nature God, [Jesus] did not consider equality with God something to be used to his own advantage; rather, he made himself nothing by taking the very nature of a servant, being made in human likeness. And being found in appearance as a man, he

humbled himself by becoming obedient to death—

even death on a cross! Therefore God exalted him to
the highest place and gave him the name that is above
every name, that at the name of Jesus every knee
should bow, in heaven and on earth and under the
earth, and every tongue acknowledge that Jesus Christ
is Lord, to the glory of God the Father.

If you want to know what a strong man is, Jesus shows
us true strength.

There's only one Man with the power and authority to
be the Fixer. And when you choose to lay down your
tough-guy facade and receive his victory on your behalf
—when you can admit you've always been the one who
needs fixing—that's a strong-man decision.

"Can we talk?"

I believe our fix-it attitude as men is wired into our sin
nature. And, in a fallen world, there's much to be fixed.
We seem to approach every problematic issue as a test of
our intelligence, strength, control, or abilities. If a
woman has a flat tire, eventually a good guy will stop for
the sole reason of saving a damsel in distress. I don't
believe there's anything wrong with this.

But if The Fixer is your sole identity, you will run into
problems. You can't rescue everyone. You can't protect

everyone. You can't fix everyone. In fact, you can't even fix yourself. But you can seek to know yourself by asking yourself why you do what you do.

A tough guy seldom if ever takes stock of his situation in life. *Introspection* isn't a word in his vocabulary. Stopping to smell the roses seems ridiculous. But a strong man seeks to understand others and where his place in the world can have the greatest impact.

Personally, I had to learn how to overcome my fix-it mentality in my marriage and with my daughters. Although my need to fix things came out in many different ways, it always seemed to be most evident right after my wife would ask me those three dreaded words: "Can we talk?"

Since being tough is always about self-preservation, tough guys have a hard time truly being attentive to anyone else. Even the problems of others ultimately become about your role as *their* fixer. And this makes true listening impossible.

One day, when I'd just walked in the door from a long day at work, my wife asked, "Can we talk?" Dutifully, I nodded and we sat down. She poured out her heart to me about several things with which she'd been struggling. Most of them concerned her job at our church and the departments she oversaw.

Five minutes into her story, as if on some internal clock I could never turn off, I knew exactly how to fix her problems. As she was still telling me about what she was wrestling with, I interrupted her. "Hold on just a second."

With my wife still sitting next to me, I grabbed my phone, dialed our executive pastor, and barked a few orders, telling him exactly what he needed to do to fix my wife's problems at her job. I glanced at my wife and smiled, my chest likely puffing out. Subconsciously, I thought, *Look at me and how I fixed this for you. Aren't you so glad you married me?*

But instead of seeing a grateful smile and hearing resounding praise and applause, I saw grief and disbelief in her eyes. As soon as I hung up, she said, "What are you doing? I didn't want you to *fix* it! I just wanted you to listen to me!" She stormed out of the room.

I sat in silence, totally confused. *So she's not glad she married me? Aren't I supposed to help her in life? Didn't I just do that? What just happened here?*

Men, if you haven't learned this lesson already, let my

story be your example of how *not* to listen. Most of the time, when your wife, girlfriend, daughter, or sister wants to talk to you, they don't want you to fix their problems. More than likely, they're asking if you'll lay aside your need to fix them, lay aside the world that revolves around you, and simply listen to their heart.

Go ahead. Ask them and see if I'm not right.

They don't have a desire for us to fix all of their problems. Rather, they long to have a safe place to share and be vulnerable. Your job as a strong man is *not* to make their words about you. Lay down your desire to fix. Learn how to become a listener.

For instance, through many years of trial and error in this regard, I now ask a short but imminently helpful question immediately after my wife or one of my daughters asks if we can talk: "Is this a fix-it conversation or a listening conversation?"

These ten words have saved me from so much confusion.

Most of the time, they'll answer that it's a listening conversation. When they're through talking through whatever issue they may be wrestling with, I'll hug them and say, "I'm sorry that you're having to deal with that. Please let me know if I can help."

They'll hug me in reply, kiss me on the cheek, and say, "Thank you for always being willing to listen." Then they'll skip away, happy and satisfied.

As a man, I don't understand their response. *Why don't they want the problem solved right then and there, especially when the solution seems so apparent?* Then I laugh under my breath, shake my head, and think, *Because that's not how God wired them, and maybe they're even stronger than me because they don't need a quick fix. I bet if I listened more, I'd learn more from them too.*

I think God made women a little less physically stronger than us because, if they weren't, they might take over the world! In so many ways, my wife is stronger than me: she is a better leader, a better friend, and a better person because she is strong enough to live a life that is beyond herself, secure enough that she doesn't need to control others, and free enough that she doesn't need everything or anyone in her world to be perfect. She knows her strengths and her weaknesses and isn't afraid to let others know them as well.

I'm not a professional-level listener by any means, but I

have learned that one of the main ingredients to the success of these conversations is that my focus is solely on my wife or kids and not on how I could help them.

Strong men lay aside their egos, rest in their identity, and freely serve others. To me, that single characteristic may best define the strong man: selfless.

Just like Thor, eventually, and just like Jesus, always.

Now, Let's Get Real

Tough guys live with an unhealthy desire to have people look to them for answers. They "need" to be needed. To admit you can't fix something or admit you don't have the answer is a sign of weakness to your tough ego.

But a strong man is comfortable in who he is and who his Father is. He doesn't need to be everyone's solution and can readily point people to the ultimate solution: a faith beyond man made tough in God.

Prayer ← last pg 34

Romans 8:26-27

And the Holy Spirit helps us in our weakness. For example, we don't know what God wants us to pray for. But the Holy Spirit prays for us with groanings that can not be expressed in words. And the father who knows all hearts knows all hearts knows what the Spirit is saying, for the Spirit pleads for us believers in harmony with God's own will.

What areas in your life do you still feel like you must have all the answers?

My <u>Prayer Life</u>. Prayer is a Relationship, not just a Religious activity.

I'm always judging the situation. I have have to talk my self out of the prayer I'm about to say. Like a guy setting in front of a laptop trying to type out an assignment. I argue with my self and then I finally get it. Oh you were trying to show me this! what importance is that, what will that do?

<u>Prayer walk</u> — why haven't I done more for my fellow Brother or Sister? It would be so easy to say oh your Physically in Prison. We don't have the <u>means</u> (<u>financial</u> resources or Biblical Knowledge

you just have to Listen

Life — your family is dependent on you
It looks bad if you don't have the answers.

TRAMA — Life creates TRAMA, not just Disaster. Like tornadoes or a life-taking event.
In trama we have to try to rationalize
attempt to explain or justify (one's own or another's behavior or attitude) with logical, plausible reasons even if these are not true or Appropriate.

Do you try to fabricate an answer in fear of looking like or admitting that you don't have an answer? If so, why?

Especially if the person asking, makes
it like — you don't know
            Should know
            why don't you know

Look like?
a man that was studying the word more.
a man that was not just Reacting to daily
life events.
a man that can stand his ground because
he had a relationship with the Lord almighty
and the Lord told him, Advised him

a man who could shed doubtful eyes
    Because he knew that there is Absolutely
knowing he could do that would turn his
heavenly father away from him.

It takes more strength to admit you don't know than it does to pretend you do. If you are willing to be strong enough to admit that you don't have all the answers and you are not the solution, what would that look like in your life?

Religious Life:
It reminds me of the first Life group
I joined with my wife. I grew up Catholic
for thirty-something years. Wife always wanted to
join. But I had this image that there was a Quiz
on your knowledge of the Bible. Or you should
have read the whole bible. There was a young couple
and one of them would ask questions that I would never
ask, I might have thought but never asked.
It would make me Look bad, or stupid.
But it was great because that question would open
up the discussion into inquiring and thoughtful
coversation with the whole group -

Idea of being stronger?
Keep a spiritual journal or diary. When the Creator of the universe tells you something in your quiet time record it. Before you forget it. The write your prayer Response If he speaks to you through Scripture, write the Scripture down and what he told you.

FIXER FOCUS VERSES

Prayer is two-way fellowship And Communication with God you speak to God, and he speaks to you. Prayer is not a one-way conversation in which you merely list everything you want God to do. Prayer includes Listening. In fact what God Says in prayer is for more important than what you say

Galatians 2:20: "I have been crucified with Christ; it is no longer I who live, but Christ lives in me; and the life which I now live in the flesh I live by faith in the Son of God, who loved me and gave Himself for me."

John 15:5: "I am the vine, you are the branches. He who abides in Me, and I in him, bears much fruit; for without Me you can do nothing."

Philippians 4:13: "I can do all things through Christ who strengthens me."

Prayer is a relationship, not just a religious activity. Its purpose is to Adjust you to God, Not to align God with your thinking. God doesn't need your prayers But he wants you to pray because of what God wants to do in And through your Life as you Pray.

THREE
THE CHEAT

When I was a senior in high school, my last-period class was history.

I didn't really see a need for history in my life. I always focused on moving forward. After all, the windshield is bigger than the rearview mirror for a reason.

Every Thursday, the teacher would review for our test on Friday. He'd set the test on his desk and go over the questions with us. He had every letter circled that coincided with the correct answer. I got very good at reading upside down. I'd work hard on Thursday to memorize the sequence of letters and be ready to ace the test the following day.

If I had worked as hard at learning the subject as I did at cheating, I would have been much more in tune with our world today. Instead, I've had to go back many times and learn what I should have learned in high school to understand current events.

Yes, I got an A in the class, but I learned nothing except how to read letters upside down.

I also got a lot of tickets that year for speeding—but I knew a way out. I'd hire a lawyer, and he could get me out of those tickets. However, my cheating the law quickly came to a halt when the police showed up in that same history class one Friday afternoon. They arrested me in the hallway for having seven warrants out for unpaid speeding tickets!

Everyone laughed at me as I was walked out of the school and was escorted into an awaiting squad car. How embarrassing. But it was just easier not to pay the tickets.

Just like it was easier not to study.

Just like it was easier to cut corners than do the right thing.

I was a tough guy, so I was a cheat. And being a cheat in the relatively small things makes it far too easy to be a cheat in the relatively big things. Had God not gotten ahold of me and changed my life, I have to imagine that my small-time cheating ways could have exploded into something much more devastating and sadly all too common for many tough guys today.

Who's Cheating?

Imagine that your everyday tough guy is having some challenges in his marriage. He's weary of putting in the necessary marital work to get through their rough patch. In fact, he's giving her the cold shoulder or the silent treatment just to show her who's boss. This tactic typically keeps him from being intimate as well, so now he's vulnerable to other distractions.

Pornography is an easy and quick release, so he gives in to its temptation. After all, who needs a partner when you have a computer screen, right?

Depending on the source, the pornography industry generates revenue anywhere between 3 to 10 billion dollars per year. Men are its primary target. Why do we fund this industry? Well, the industry consists of tough guys dominating weak women.

Tough guys like to—or need to—be seen as sexual macho machines desired by the female race. That sounds exaggerated, and it may be to an extent, but the tough guy always takes the easy way out. He prefers the path of least resistance. It's much easier to watch pornography and masturbate to a made-up fantasy than to romance his wife and stay true to her. It's much easier to flirt with his co-worker than to stay true to his godly character. It's much easier to cheat than to do the right thing.

Cheating on his wife in this manner drives this tough guy further away from his wife. Using porn is a selfish action and kills intimacy between him and pretty much anyone he's very close with—including God.

While intimacy decreases at home, then comes a quick glance from a co-worker or acquaintance, and the tough guy responds. Then she laughs, affirming his attention. It seems innocent and somewhat exciting, so he goes with it. Pretty soon, he has a new relationship, and she likes him.

Of course, she knows nothing about him, but what he lets her see she likes. This new relationship is exciting, easy, and fun and gives him something to look forward to. So, the tough guy continues on. Before long, he's investing in this new relationship, and she seems to reciprocate.

The hardest thing about the relationship is hiding it

from his wife and those around him (just like his porn usage). But even that seems exciting and daring. It almost makes him feel alive again. After all, life is all about him, and this validates that premise.

If life is about making himself happy—of course, his insecurity tells him it is—then any attention, affection, or feeling he can get is right.

But, all the while, he's completely stopped investing in his marriage. His wife knows he's pulled away. She can feel the abandonment. She begins to operate out of insecurity and is getting suspicious about something. He's fooled himself into thinking he isn't doing anything wrong because he hasn't crossed over into a sexual relationship with his new interest. (Again, this echoes the tough guy's self-rationalization over his porn usage too.)

However, a sexual encounter with his new romantic interest is very likely just around the corner.

But he's the tough guy. He believes he's in control. He believes he can handle the situation.

But he can't.

It's a trap, and he's too blind in his insecurities to see what's coming.

In fact, he's so tough that he's spent the last few minutes trying to dislodge the notion that this story may be about him.

Why Do Tough Guys Cheat?

Tough guys cheat on their wives and children, tearing apart their families. Tough guys cheat on their business partners, not only ruining their own professional lives but those of many others. Tough guys cheat on their bodies by not taking care of themselves, leading to an early death. They allow their moods and emotions to lead them. Consequently, they take the path of least resistance. Tough guys give in.

Why?

From a lack of discipline.

DeMarcus Ware was an NFL defensive end for the Dallas Cowboys who went on to help the Denver Broncos win Super Bowl 50. That man can pursue a quarterback like few other defensive linemen. On every play, he had one goal: to get to the quarterback. Nothing distracted him from accomplishing that goal.

But his pursuit of sacking an NFL quarterback didn't start on Sunday at kickoff. Rather, it began on the first day of his summer preseason workouts. It started in the gym, when he was working hard to strengthen his body. It started many years before that, when he decided to live his life in such a way that all of his disciplines would move him toward his goal. How he lived his life determined his readiness. His achievements in Super Bowl 50 were a completion of years of right decisions and disciplines to get him there.

Joe Frazier, the famous boxer, has been quoted as saying, "What you do in the early morning hours is illuminated in the ring of lights." Joe understood that he didn't become a great boxer overnight. He became a great boxer every morning he woke up and chose to train and discipline his mind and body for that goal.

Similarly, to be the strong men God has called us to be means that we must make conscious, daily decisions to discipline ourselves. We must constantly and consistently pursue him *and* the one he has given us in our wives. After thirty-two years of marriage, I am still pursuing my wife's heart. I want to be in constant pursuit of her. I should not let anything distract me from my goal. Every morning I wake up, I chose to pursue her.

I want to be physically disciplined by taking care of my body as a thank you to her for marrying me. I want to be mentally disciplined to keep my eyes and focus on her and not be distracted by what is thrown in front of me. I will not allow anything to stop me from pursuing my bride. I will be relentless and show my strength and discipline to anyone or anything that will try to stop me. A strong man will fight for his marriage and never grow weary of the investment.

So, you tell me which one takes more strength: the discipline and decision to be in constant pursuit of your marriage or the passivity to be distracted by outside influences that take away from your disciplines?

People have asked Dana and me why we have such a great marriage. It hasn't always been great. I have acted the tough guy too many times to count. But when people ask us what our secret is, we respond, "There is no secret. We fight all the time."

I know how that sounds, but it's the truth. Let me explain.

We have a phrase we use. We want to be "hand-to-hand, face-to-face, chest-to-chest, and heart-to-heart."

Nothing between us.

But when something does try to pull us apart, we fight to get it out of the way and get back in rhythm with each other. If something happens in our relationship, even the smallest bump, we both feel it immediately, and we refuse to let it take up roots.

We fight to stay close to each other, hand-to-hand, face-to-face, chest-to-chest, heart-to-heart.

How Jesus Models Discipline

Jesus knew what it meant to be disciplined and focused. He wasn't a tough guy. He was the strong man of conviction we ought to emulate.

We glimpse Jesus's disciplined humanity when he paused in the garden of Gethsemane. "He went a little farther and fell on his face, and prayed, saying, 'O My Father, if it is possible, let this cup pass from Me; Nevertheless, not as I will, but as You will'" (Matthew 26:39 NKJV).

Christ's humanity shows up here and tries to distract him from his ultimate goal. Jesus acknowledges the distraction. "My flesh doesn't want this Father. Is there any way around this? But I won' t let it stop me from the pursuit of my goal." What was his goal? What was Jesus pursuing? The cross?

No.

Hebrews 12 tells us that he endured the cross for the *joy* that was set before him. The cross was something he had to go through to get what he wanted. What did he pursue? What joy was he after? What was he so focused on that nothing would deter him? What did he pursue from the first steps he took as a child to the steps he took up Calvary?

It was his bride. His church. It was you.

From the time he left his heavenly throne, entered this world through the body of a virgin, and was laid in a manger by the hands of a carpenter, he had one goal. Every decision he made, every discipline he had, was to keep him in line with his pursuit: to be your savior.

He longs to save you from yourself. He wants to show you how to replace your tough-guy exterior with a strong-man interior. He can help you overcome any of your cheating ways, from the smallest of issues to the biggest of problems.

Integrity and character are defined by what we do when no one is around. Integrity and character are built by making the right decisions every day not to cut corners and not to give in to our fleshly desires.

A strong man will do the right thing because it is what is

in him and who he is. It's not about the insecure need to impress and receive praise. Cheating is often easy, risky, and exciting. It's easier to cheat on your taxes than to be a man of integrity. It can be easy, risky, and exciting to look at something on the internet you know you shouldn't be looking at.

Integrity, character, and doing the right thing are fueled by the strength of a godly man, not the toughness of a cheat. The path of passivity promises satisfaction to the flesh. But, in the end, you see the lie that you believed and then comes the destruction.

Whatever the case, stop letting the whisper of cheating lead you down the path of passivity to a destructive end. Start being fueled by making decisions based on who you are as a strong man of God. Let integrity, character, and honor flow through you as you pursue your goal. Let nothing stop you.

Then, one day, you too will stand in the Super Bowl arena of heaven as all the saints of old cheer for you. Then you will hear your heavenly father say, "Well done, thy good and faithful servant. You fought the good fight, you finished the race, and you have kept the faith. Enter into your eternal reward."

· · ·

Now, Let's Get Real

Cheating on something or someone is nothing more than taking a shortcut toward immediate gratification. The temptation to cheat is a voice that says, "Do this and you will get there quicker." It is a promise to get you to a legitimate need for gratification through illegitimate means.

Temptation always points us toward a God-given desire to be accepted or satisfied. But the instrument to get you there will always leave you feeling shameful, dirty, and with a need to hide your sin. Tough guys go the way of the world and are looking for the immediate fix. It takes true strength to go to God and allow him to truly fulfill you.

What areas in your life are you unfulfilled and susceptible to a quick fix?

In what areas have you stopped pursuing God's will for your life?

What would it look like in your life to start pursuing truth and fulfillment through your relationship with God and stop cheating on yourself and others?

THE CHEAT FOCUS VERSES

Galatians 5:16, 22–26: "I say then: Walk in the Spirit, and you shall not fulfill the lust of the flesh. For the flesh lusts against the Spirit, and the Spirit against the flesh; and these are contrary to one another, so that you do not do the things that you wish. . . . The fruit of the Spirit is love, joy, peace, longsuffering, kindness, goodness, faithfulness, gentleness, self-control. Against such there is no law. And those who are Christ's have crucified the flesh with its passions and desires. If we live in the Spirit, let us also walk in the Spirit. Let us not become conceited, provoking one another, envying one another."

Micah 6:8: "He has shown you, O man, what is good; And what does the Lord require of you But to do justly, To love mercy, And to walk humbly with your God?"

FOUR

THE ORPHAN

·

Have you ever been to an orphanage in a third-world country?

It's an experience you'll never forget.

Dana and I support an orphanage in Chiapas, Mexico, through Mexico Ministries. We have watched many kids grow up in this orphanage. We try to go at least once a year, if not more. But, regardless of how often we visit, the scene is always the same. The younger kids come running up to us, craving affection and attention. They squeeze us until we can hardly breathe. Then they perform for us, showing how well they can play ball or dance or draw. It's all about showing us how good they are so we will love them, accept them, and hopefully want to adopt them.

Unfortunately, most orphanages in Mexico do not allow for adoption because of sex-trading and sex-trafficking crimes. So, most of the children are there until they reach eighteen years of age. But this doesn't stop the little ones from hoping and trying to get our attention.

Then there are the older ones.

They've already been through the performance phase and have somewhat given up. They stay in the back, leaning against a wall, making sure to keep their distance. They want no part of the hope for a better family. They are simply waiting until they have to leave and will try to find a way to survive outside the walls of their orphanage.

Often unknown to them, so many tough guys are just like these older orphans. In fact, we're all born with an orphan wound.

The Orphan Wound

By definition, an orphan is someone who has lost or has been separated from their parents and is without a home. When sin entered the garden of Eden, Adam and Eve were separated from their Father. It's important to know that God did not abandon them; their sin separated them. It was their choice that detached them from the family. Since that time, every human who has been born came from the seed of that sin. Thus, we are all born into sin, separated from our Father. We're all spiritual orphans at birth.

Depending on your earthly experiences, the orphan wound can be enhanced or softened.

For example, I honor my dad, thank him for giving me his name, and appreciate all that he did for me growing up. But I'm not his biological son, and he didn't exactly parent from a place of love. He was a quiet and hard man who ruled by expectations and his belt on my backside. Then there was the occasional beating at home.

I always had a nagging feeling that I didn't seem to belong to anyone or anything, so I did what any orphan would do. I performed. I'd be the best athlete I could be, the best at whatever I could do, in hopes of attracting attention and getting accepted.

I was a pretty good athlete and got some attention with my skills. I wasn't an ugly guy, necessarily, so I was able to get the girls. I did get attention, but it never seemed to be enough to free me from my orphan mentality. Just like the older kids in Mexico, I began to withdraw and believe that my survival was solely up to me.

Of course, only tough guys survive. And man was I tough. I didn't need anyone. But, oddly enough, the nagging desire to be accepted has never gone away, even though I'm a grown man. I often find myself still trying to perform for attention.

For some tough guys, this happens when you're trying to be the best so your boss notices you. You still "need" to be noticed and accepted. When you think you may be rejected, the tough guy comes out. The tough guy says, "I don't care whether you like me or not. I don't need you. The heck with you and what you think. I reject you as a person and a peer before you can reject me." Every time you sense rejection, it confirms your suspicion that you really are alone and it's up to you to make your own way. So, the tough guy rises to the occasion and bullies his way forward, leaving bodies in his wake.

An orphan mentality says you are alone in the world and solely responsible for your provision, protection, and position in life. Self-preservation rules your actions. Driven by fear, tough guys act like orphans who've never learned to trust others.

The orphan doesn't know who their father is and lives as if they are alone. You live thinking you were and are rejected. You were and are alone. With that nagging thought comes a deep, God-given desire to be accepted. So, you live your life in a constant state of seeking someone to accept you. This ever-searching radar leaves you vulnerable to so many bad things.

Why do boys get into gangs? Because they are looking for acceptance. This need is a legitimate desire given by God but perverted by the enemy. Most young boys who would join a gang of any kind typically have no fatherly role model, and they fall prey to an older guy who will give them attention, protection, and acceptance.

Men have marital affairs because they don't feel fully accepted, so they are constantly searching for the next acceptance they believe will complete them. The least amount of attention feels very good to them, and they are lured toward the hope of finding something they think is missing from their lives. It doesn't matter that their wives may love them unconditionally. It isn't enough. They are lacking and they know it. Often, they do blame their wife—until they find themselves in the arms of another woman who won't fulfill them either. And then another and another.

Men with orphan mentalities will also parent from that emotional platform. A father who was never really accepted in sports will push his son or daughter toward sports, secretly hoping for the satisfaction of admiration he never got in school. A father will push his son toward unhealthy relationships with girls so he can live out another hope of acceptance that he never received. An orphaned father will spoil his children and make sure they appear to be perfect so they will get accepted.

If someone or some organization does not accept them, the father will turn tough guy on those who have rejected his children. Since the father is living vicariously through his child, *he's* the one getting rejected— and we know how a tough guy handles rejection. You've probably seen the scenario where a father goes off and screams at an umpire over what he thinks is a bad call, or a dad yelling at a coach for not playing his child enough in the game. The child doesn't seem to care nearly as much as the parent. Why would he? It's the parents' show, and the child is just a pawn in the parent's game.

The issue isn't with your child or the ump. The issue isn't with your wife. The issue isn't what group you associate yourself with. The issue is the acceptance that you as an orphan need but aren't receiving. And the foundational issue is your relationship with your father —your heavenly Father, that is.

For such an orphan, that nagging feeling of not having

enough love, of not really being accepted to the level you know you need, is always there whether you are conscious of it or not. The emotional prison you live in is called *Rejection State Penitentiary*. Most of your energy is used up trying to break out of that place. Let me go back to what I said earlier: This insatiable desire for acceptance was actually given to you by your Father. Is it a cruel joke he's played on us? He gives us a desire he knows we can never fill? What the heck?

Let me explain. When Satan entered the garden, he convinced Eve that she was incomplete. He told her that she still needed the fruit from the tree to be everything she was supposed to be. Though she was already made in her Father's image and was perfect, Satan tricked her into thinking she needed something else. Sin entered the garden, and Satan has been showing us insufficient apples ever since. He knows the things of this world will never complete us and that we will be miserable trying anything and everything he brings our way. But as long as he can hold our attention with the possibilities of worldly fulfillment, he keeps us from the ultimate Truth.

Yes, God gave us the desire to be accepted.

No, there is never going to be enough in this world to

fulfill that desire.

And no, you cannot overcome that desire, nor fill it yourself.

So what's the deal?

The freeing truth is this: We have already been adopted by a Father who is not just a good Father but also a King who desires to have a personal and daily relationship with you.

And this King prefers to be called Daddy.

Abba, Father

Paul wrote about God's name preference in Romans 8:15–17: "For you did not receive the spirit of bondage again to fear, but you received the Spirit of adoption by whom we cry out, 'Abba, Father.' The Spirit Himself bears witness with our spirit that we are children of God, and if children, then heirs—heirs of God and joint heirs with Christ" (NKJV).

If my dad is a King, then I have everything I will ever need just being his son. As my King, he provides for me. As my King, he has an army that protects me. As my King, he has given me a place at the royal table so I have a position of prominence the world could never give me.

Why would I not want to take that position and be a son in *that* family?

The only father who will ever be able to satisfy your desire for full acceptance is the One who gave you that desire. God gave you that desire knowing that he is the only One who can fulfill it. God's desire from the moment you were conceived is that he be your Father and that you be his son.

When you begin to glimpse the truth that you are the son of the Most High God, everything in your life changes. You stop falling prey to substitutes and you start learning what life as a son can truly be. The orphan patterns are still there, but slowly they begin to be replaced by the truth of who you are. The lure of a flirting female isn't going to work because you no longer have the acceptance radar pinging. The need to be a part of something will begin to subside with the revelation that you are *already* a part of something great. You have found something that is working for the first time.

You don't want the counterfeit. Why would you want to remain an orphan when you could be a prince? Why would you want to stay enslaved when you're already free?

. . .

Adopted as Sons and Daughters

In Ephesians 1:4–5, Paul wrote, "In love he predestined us for adoption to sonship through Jesus Christ." We no longer have to remain orphans, but so many tough guys —even tough-guy Christians like I was and can still be— don't realize their sonship. Two stories are stark reminders to me of this truth.

On January 1, 1863, President Abraham Lincoln signed the Emancipation Proclamation, but many slaves remained in bondage for *years* after this given freedom. Why? Because they didn't know about it! Some chose to stay in bondage because they didn't trust that their freedom was real.

Free men *chose* to remain slaves.

Likewise, we often don't realize we have been set free from the bondage of orphanhood. Or we don't believe we have been adopted. That was me for forty years. I couldn't believe I had a Father who loved me and would take care of me.

A personal story echoes this sad truth.

My wife and I were asked to meet a couple at a very nice restaurant in Dallas, one of the top steakhouses in the city. I was very excited. I like beef! I'd been looking forward to that day all week. On my way home to get my wife, I passed by at least twenty drive-through hamburger joints. After picking her up, we drove by another twenty-plus fast-food hamburger places.

We were never remotely tempted to pull into one of those places.

We knew we were getting the best and we didn't have to settle. We also knew that dining at any of those restaurants would cost us something, but we had an invitation to the best restaurant in town *and* the meal was paid for!

Why would I settle for something that would only leave me wanting more, wasn't healthy for me, and was going to cost me something?

Tough guys haven't accepted the fact that they can be or have been adopted by the King. Strength comes from the realization that there is a King who is looking for those he can adopt. This King will give all the protection his Kingdom offers—no need for tough guys any longer. This King has everything a man will ever need. No need to ever worry about having enough. He gives you a place at his table: a position of royalty. You are free to roam the land in the security of who you are because of who your Daddy is.

When I finally and fully believed in my sonship, I learned that when orphans are adopted, they can trust that their provision, protection, and position comes from their place in their new family. But I am still learning what it means to live like an heir to the family of God, with all of its unassailable family rights.

When I began to understand who I was as God's son and who he is as my Father, I changed how I parent. I became a father who wants his children to experience what I have. I realized that my duty is to point my kids to the Father I have and see them begin to excel as sons and daughters, not of David Vestal, but of God the Father. I do my best not to use my kids to try to satisfy my unhealthy needs. I work to actually become a reflection of my Father.

From this position, your kids can make a mistake and you will be there to pick them up and love them through it because *you* are loved despite *your* mistakes. Your kids can be rejected without you feeling like you're being rejected. You will love them through it, all the while being able to tell them how much you love them and, even more, how much they are unconditionally loved by their Father. Instead of using your kids to pacify your orphan thirst, you actually get to be a part of watching your kids become who God has called them to be and do what God has called them to do—and that is *very* satisfying.

Leave your fortress of solitude.

Venture out into the land that has been provided for you.

Walk in the identity that has been given to you.

Come to the table and take your seat as a prince in the King's Castle, a son of God Most High.

You're no longer an orphan, so live as his son.

Now, Let's Get Real

By definition, an orphan is someone who has lost or has been separated from his or her parents and are without a home. When sin entered the garden of Eden, Adam and Eve were separated from their Father. We are all born with sin and separated from God. But He hasn't abandoned us. He made a way for us to be adopted into His family. But, unless we know this and are willing to accept this adoption, we will live as orphans. An orphan lives in rejection and believes the lie that he is alone and his position, protection, and provision are up to him.

How does a fear of rejection and a fear of failure still operate in your life today?

Name a time when you felt like you had to perform for approval and acceptance?

How can you live in an understanding that you are not an orphan but are loved unconditionally and accepted versus feeling rejected?

THE ORPHAN FOCUS VERSES

Romans 8:15–17: "For you did not receive the spirit of bondage again to fear, but you received the Spirit of adoption by whom we cry out, 'Abba, Father.' The Spirit Himself bears witness with our spirit that we are children of God, and if children, then heirs—heirs of God and joint heirs with Christ."

Ephesians 1:3–6: "Blessed be the God and Father of our Lord Jesus Christ, who has blessed us with every spiritual blessing in the heavenly places in Christ, just as He chose us in Him before the foundation of the world, that we should be holy and without blame before Him in love, having predestined us to adoption as sons by Jesus Christ to Himself, according to the good pleasure of His will, to the praise of the glory of His grace, by which He made us accepted in the Beloved."

2 Corinthians 6:18: "I will be a Father to you, And you shall be My sons and daughters, Says the Lord Almighty."

FIVE

THE CONTROLLER

I've punched my fair share of walls and thrown things in a fit, all the while not knowing the reason behind my rages. Have you had similar experiences?

Maybe you haven't punched a wall—or a person—but you've lost control. Ironically, these out-of-control experiences are most often caused by a fear of losing control.

As gasoline fuels an engine through combustible explosions, so too does fear fuel a tough guy's actions. Like me, you may fear being found out, being hurt, not getting what's owed you, losing your job, losing a loved one, or just losing period. Fear always causes a reaction. With the passing of time and at least some maturity, I now know that my punching and fits of rage were often best understood as the result of fear.

When fear is the motivator, tough guys are the responder.

You Have More to Fear Than Fear Itself

Terrorism is rooted in getting the public to believe that something terrible is about to happen. They perform random acts of violence to get us to believe that another violent act is imminent. Fear spreads like a virus. Terrorists' primary weapon is fear, and a fear-mongering enemy can do as much damage as the act of violence itself.

If you believe that something is about to happen, you will act on that belief.

For instance, sporting goods stores have seen large spikes in "Prepper Supplies," supplies that are deemed necessary to survive a doomsday episode. Hundreds of websites are now dedicated to doomsday-prepper supplies. This movement is rooted in the fear that something cataclysmic is about to happen and a person better act now before the unthinkable occurs.

Again, fear causes a reaction.

Now, ask yourself: What causes you to yell and scream and lose your temper?

It's not because you're so tough that nobody should challenge the great and mighty man you are. You may present yourself as the king of your jungle, so you beat your chest and roar. But the reason you want everyone to show you due respect is so they will fear you. Through that fear, you can control *them*.

A lion's roar can be heard up to five miles away. He does this to scare away other animals. It's his way of signaling, "I'm in control, and you better not challenge me." He intentionally uses the fear that his roar produces to control others.

How does the enemy control you? The same way: by keeping you in bondage to fear. Peter said it well in a memorable verse from the Bible: "Be sober, be vigilant; because your adversary the devil walks about like a roaring lion, seeking whom he may devour. Resist him, steadfast in the faith" (1 Peter 5:8–9).

Fear is heard within the enemy's roar that says, "You are about to be rejected again. You are about to fail again. You are about to be hurt again. You are about to be exposed as the fraud you know you are unless you do something. Get it under control, man, or risk losing it all."

This is how that fear often played out for me. If I am in control of my space, then I can decide who comes into my world. Therefore, I won't ever be rejected, hurt, wounded, or exposed—as long as I am in control. Of course, I couldn't venture outside of that territorial box lest I lose everything. So I created a fortress of solitude to make sure nothing bad happens ever again. And I growled at any who would dare approach my cage.

What kind of a life is that?

Who wants to live in fear of losing everything and gaining nothing but maybe an ulcer?

Fear Before Faith

Fear is the belief that something is about to happen. But, wait a minute. Isn't faith also the belief that something is about to happen?

Fear says something bad is coming. Faith says something good has already come. The only difference is the object of your belief.

But it seems as if we default to fear. We live in fear much more than we live in faith. Why?

Faith is the belief that God is working on your behalf and that he will show up and do great and mighty things. But fear has convinced us that we are not worthy enough for God to show up, so he won't; therefore, we're on our own (the orphan's foundational belief).

We think, *Oh, God will show up for our pastor or our teacher or that guy I know who is really holy. But me? No. You see, I know who I am. I know what kind of a sinner I am. I know the things I've done in the dark and terrible places I let my mind wander. I am definitely not worthy of God showing up. So, yeah, fear it is.*

We let fear reign because we're afraid we'll be forever rejected at the core of our being. You may experience all kinds of acceptance on the surface. You may even enjoy enough acceptance by those who really know you. But there's a third level all tough guys have and that all tough guys would be terrified to share.

What You're Hiding

There are three parts to this illustration: the overt, the covert, and the pervert.

The top layer is your overt side, what you allow everyone to see. It's you at your best. You wear your pasted-on Christian smile and you're as pleasant as can

be. You're charming and nice and are in full performance mode, hoping people will like you.

The middle layer is your covert side, the side that few
see. Your family sees you when you're not smiling. This
is the place where your anger swells and explodes, often
accidentally appearing in your overt side, though that's
never your intention. The covert side is where you let
down your performance mind-set and allow yourself to
be yourself: the grouchy, mean, and, at times, cantan-
kerous tough guy all men can sometimes become.

Beneath the overt top layer and the covert middle layer
sits the lowest layer. The pervert layer is the dark room
in the cellar of your soul that you don't allow anyone
into. You know what's in there. It's your worst thoughts
and deeds of the past. It's your dark and ugly side. Its
pus and poisonous stench constantly remind you just
how bad you really are. You don't even like to go there
much less let anyone else peek inside. When you do
sneak in, you don't stay long. You keep the doors locked
tight and the lights off.

The fear of someone finding out the truth about you is
really what fuels the tough guy's covert side. This fear
keeps him living in constant terror that someone will
discover who he really is. He knows what is down there,

and he knows it's controlling him. This is the one room he really has no control over. It scares him and keeps him emotionally drained, which makes for a very miserable person. Then that misery and stink find their way up into his overt side, at times causing the tough guy to react out of fear that someone will find out the truth.

So what do you do with something you can't control and, at times, even controls you?

The Finishing Work of *Tetelestai*

Let me share some amazing news.

God did not send his Son to die for your overt side. Neither did he send his Son to die for your covert side. God the Father sent his Son, Jesus Christ, to die on a cross for your pervert side.

That cellar of past sins has been taken care of.

Jesus died so you can be set free from that control. There is no condemnation for those who have received Jesus and believe in what he has done for them (Romans 8:1).

Jesus's last word on the cross was *tetelestai* (John 19:30). That word is the greatest word ever spoken by any man on the planet, past, present, or future. We don't have an

English word to describe it, so we use three words to try to explain it. In our Bibles, *tetelestai* is most often translated "It is finished!" That means paid in full. That means the debt has been forgiven and you are free from its terms. The debt of your perverse sins has been paid. They no longer have control over you.

The blood of Jesus has run like a river through your basement and cleaned you out so there's nothing to hide. You are free to live the life God has called you to live. The tough guy doesn't reign there any longer. Fear doesn't own that space in you any longer.

Will God really show up for you?

He already has.

Your fear can now be replaced with faith. You can call on his character instead of reacting in rage to your insecurities. Instead of hiding in your fear and worry, you can live in his strength and walk in his light. Where fear has paralyzed you, faith now propels you, moving you beyond your walls of fearful control and into his kingdom.

Fear is the belief that something is about to happen. Faith is the belief that something has *already* happened. While fear fuels the engine of a tough guy, faith fuels the engine of a strong man. The strong man believes the word of God: "Be strong in the Lord and in the power of His might" (Ephesians 6:10 NKJV).

Never Surrender

Have you ever thought about laying down your defenses and surrendering to God? I know it's not easy. It takes great courage and strength.

In the police academy, I was taught never to surrender in a fight. Surrender would most likely get you killed or, at least, captured so *never* surrender. And I never did.

I may have been wrong, but I'd never admit that. In fact, I'd fight someone before risking losing or looking bad. I may have gone down with the ship in a fight, but I wouldn't quit. We even had a motto in our family: "Vestals never give up."

Yes, there can be some value in your tenacity, but, in the kingdom of God, surrender means you *gain* everything by *giving up* control. It's not easy, and tough guys seldom if ever do it.

It takes strength to lay down your defense mechanisms and begin trusting in a Father you can't see. It takes strength to give up control and begin to believe there is a greater plan than just your survival.

That was my mind-set, my fear, for years—until God questioned me: "David, was the cross not enough for you? Was my Son not enough for you? Do I need to have a second sacrifice for your sins? Do you think you need to do something more to rid yourself of your sins? Do you honestly think you can or need to add to the cross and what I have done for you?"

Ouch.

But that's where I was. Maybe it's where you are now.

Though we may never say it out loud, our lives are saying that what Jesus did on the cross has covered our pastor's sins and our teacher's sins and the sins of the religious fanatic at work. But it wasn't enough for *us*.

No, God. You have done so much for me that I am not worthy of it.

Well, that's right.

None of us are.

Including your pastor or teacher or even that religious fanatic.

Remember: *tetelestai*.

· · ·

Now, Let's Get Real

The greatest driver behind the dynamic of fear is the need to control. A fear of failure or a fear of rejection will cause a man to attempt to control his surroundings. If we can control our surroundings, then we can mitigate the risk of failing or being rejected. Control becomes a survival tactic, and we will do whatever we need to do in order to survive with our insecurity.

But a strong man understands who is really in control. True security is found in a God-given assurance that eliminates the need to prove the value of who you are or the rightness of what you do. The absence of fear is produced by the total belief that God is in control. He loves you and will never leave you or forsake you.

In what way have you allowed the need to control to manipulate your actions?

How do you let fear control you, and how do you use fear to control others?

What fears and concerns can you give to God today that could free you from a need to intimidate?

THE CONTROLLER FOCUS VERSES

Galatians 2:20: "I have been crucified with Christ; it is no longer I who live, but Christ lives in me; and the life which I now live in the flesh I live by faith in the Son of God, who loved me and gave Himself for me."

Proverbs 3:5–6: "Trust in the Lord with all your heart, And lean not on your own understanding; In all your ways acknowledge Him, And He shall direct your paths."

1 John 4:18: "There is no fear in love; but perfect love casts out fear, because fear involves torment. But he who fears has not been made perfect in love."

SIX

THE CON MAN

U p until my first triathlon experience, I had always desired to complete a triathlon. Knowing I shouldn't start by attacking the entire race, I entered myself into a mini-triathlon: a half-mile swim, a twelve-mile bike ride, and a three-mile run.

Because of my policing background and regular exercise regimen, I felt as if I were fairly ready. Still, I trained for three months, actually completing the full swim, bike, and run at least twice a week at my athletic club. I knew without a doubt that I could complete the race.

On the day of the event, my wife and I drove out to the lake park where the race was to take place. I quickly noticed that I was one of the older entrants, but my confidence remained high. This was a *mini*-triathlon, after all.

Then I gazed upon the first leg.

The lake water had whitecaps. The wind had to have been blowing in excess of twenty-five miles per hour for the waves to be showing off that way. In fact, a race official announced, "Today's swim will be more challenging than normal given the wind. If you're not confident about the swim portion, *please* wait for another event."

I heard his voice while surveying the rough waters. I still believed I could easily swim a half-mile, even though I had only trained indoors. *How difficult could it be?* I reasoned with myself. As I surveyed the other swimmers, I thought, *I'm definitely tougher than the average guy.* Then I glanced at my wife, who waved to me. *And I'm definitely* not *going to be seen as a failure in her eyes. Not today, Vestal. You have to do this.*

Like so many of my other experiences in life, I chose to bull my way through.

Not a Good Idea

The whistle sounded. The first group ran into the water. The first buoy they had to reach was about two hundred yards away, but so many were faltering. I couldn't believe it! I watched the lifeguards pull people from the water one by one as they struggled to swim the white-capped waters. Contestants were being pulled to safety at an alarming pace.

As I stood there thinking, *Maybe this isn't such a good idea*, the next whistle blew. I ran into the water.

This isn't anything like what I was expecting.

All around me, swimmers were inadvertently kicking me in the head and pushing me under. We were a school of fish just trying to survive.

When I finally made it to the first buoy, I turned and was immediately taken under by a large wave. I came up gasping for air. I tried to compose myself. I didn't want to look like I was having trouble. Not me!

Just then, a lifeguard pulled up next to me on a Jet Ski and asked, "Are you OK?"

I grabbed hold of the Jet Ski and paused to catch my breath. As politely as I could, I replied, "Ma'am, my wife's just over there on the bank watching me. I'm not going to quit."

She didn't say anything in reply, but she let me go.

I pushed off and started to swim again. It was only a few seconds until I went under again.

Then my body started to panic. I couldn't catch my breath. I couldn't calm down. I wasn't able to get enough air to even put my face in the water and stroke. I was in deep trouble and started to think, *I just might drown.*

About that time, the same lifeguard showed up again. "Grab my hand, sir." It was an order, not a question. She pulled me up next to the Jet Ski.

I hung on and attempted to regain my composure. As soon as my breath returned, I was going to sweet-talk her into letting me finish the race again.

She must have known what I was about to do because she preempted me. "You're through for the day."

"No, I'm—"

I was interrupted by my feet touching the ground. The entire time I'd been arguing with her, she'd been pulling me to shore and I hadn't known it.

Standing up defeated in shallow water, I walked slowly toward the bank from where Dana had been watching. All I could think was, *I didn't even make the first leg of the race!*

She hugged me and comforted me.

As I sat there with her, recounting what just happened, I looked at her and said, "Honey, this may be the dumbest thing I have ever done!" We laughed. Then we collected ourselves and got out of there.

My bullheaded toughness had almost killed me. I had conned myself into thinking I was able to accomplish something I wasn't prepared for and it had almost cost me my life.

The tough guy is such a good con man that he even cons himself.

Hard Heads

NFL players are well-known tough guys. They push themselves beyond their physical limits and hope their bodies can hold up. But most pay a severe penalty for the abuse as signs of wear and tear begin to show up as early as age thirty-five.

After NFL Hall of Fame guard Mike Webster died of a heart attack, Dr. Bennett Omalu was tasked with performing his autopsy. Over the last several years of his life, Webster had grown increasingly difficult to deal with due to mental disorders. During the autopsy, Dr. Omalu found signs of brain trauma and linked the damage to the excessive blows to the head Webster had taken during his career. This problem became known as Chronic Traumatic Encephalopathy, now commonly known as CTE.

Consequently, the NFL concussion protocol has had to change at a fast pace to keep up with athletes believing they can use their heads as ramming tools against their opponents. The medical profession has also had to come in, along with the legal side, to instill rules to protect athletes who are pushing themselves beyond their limits.

And it's not just NFL players who con themselves. I'm willing to bet that a majority of athletes convince themselves that no one can stop them. It's not true, but they believe that in order to achieve peak performance. Professional athletes push themselves beyond their physical limits because they have conned themselves into believing they're somewhat invincible.

But they're not invincible. They're human, so they're vulnerable.

For instance, did you know that a woodpecker would make a better NFL player—at least insofar as crashing helmets goes? The woodpecker carves out its home by repeatedly ramming its head into a tree. Why doesn't it suffer brain damage? The woodpecker has the unique ability to wrap its tongue around its brain, thus cushioning the brain from each blow.

Humans weren't made to use our heads for such an exercise, yet that doesn't stop an NFL player from talking himself into believing he can and he should.

But what a price to pay, even for the most expensive of contracts.

Tough guys have always believed the con of invincibility. But there's a worse con: believing a lie so deeply that it becomes truth.

The Con within the Con

Of course, the word *con* is short for convincing. You are actually convincing one party that one event is taking place while orchestrating another event entirely. A con is designed to make you think one thing while something else is happening behind the scenes.

If you've seen *Ocean's Eleven*, you've seen a con within a con. Heist expert Danny Ocean (George Clooney) has been recently released from prison. By the time he exits, his next heist has already been planned. He plans to rob Terry Benedict (Andy Garcia) of $150 million by taking down three casinos in Las Vegas, all of which Benedict owns: The Bellagio, The Mirage, and The MGM.

Ocean hires ten experts to help with the heist and convinces them that it will be a great score and everyone will get rich. But Ocean is actually conning his own team. Ocean's real desire is to frame Benedict because Benedict has taken Danny's ex-wife. Danny wants her back. So Danny cons his men into conning Benedict into believing several cons in order to get the girl.

It's a fun movie to watch because we love to watch master cons at work. But it's an entirely different story with real-life con men.

As a former police officer, I've come across a lot of con artists. They are really good at making you believe their story is true even though they *know* they're lying to you. They're so practiced at their con that it comes naturally to them. Still, they know they're lying to you. They may even know that *you* know they're lying to you—and they'll still try to con you.

But then there are those con artists who lie to you and actually believe they're telling the truth. They're conning you, but they're also conning themselves. They've bought into their own lie and believe their altered reality is truth. These are some of the most dangerous people I've ever been around. You cannot convince them that they're wrong.

And if they fully believe they're in the right, they will do anything—*anything*—to maintain that illusion.

I Can Handle It

For example, I had a friend who had hired an attractive personal assistant. He enjoyed her personality, and she was good at her job. After a while, she could even predict what he'd need. She also encouraged him every chance she could and made him feel special with her daily compliments.

Now, my friend was the definition of a tough guy. Everyone looked up to him. He was a big guy, and handsome, successful, and fun to be around. But his need for attention and his insecurities made him vulnerable to possible relational traps.

I once asked him about his relationship with his assistant.

"It's a very professional relationship," he replied.

I didn't believe him. Every time I saw him in her presence, he lit up like a Christmas tree. I noticed his behavior changing toward her. He began to complain more about his wife.

As I dug deeper into the relationship, he became defensive. "Listen, David, I know my limitations, and I can handle myself. Me being alone with her is not a big deal, and I won't cross any lines."

That's a con.

My friend had conned himself into thinking he was tough enough to handle that tempting situation. He couldn't see the danger in the process. He couldn't see past the present and into a future where the repercussions of his actions could cause him to lose everything.

The hardest thing about such a scenario is that these tough-guy cons *believe* themselves. They don't just give a casual nod to their thoughts, feelings, and actions. They wholeheartedly agree with their assessment of their situation.

Thankfully, my friend came to his senses. He released his secretary before anything unfortunate occurred. But this scenario far too often ends in an affair and eventual divorce because the tough guy gives in to the temptation he was so sure he could avoid.

My wife doesn't trust me to be alone with an attractive female. I don't blame her. In my former tough-guy days, I would have conned myself into believing that such a situation was harmless and I could handle it. After all, it felt good to be alone with an attractive female while still believing I was in control. But, in learning to be a strong man, I learned to admit my weaknesses and know my limitations.

Tough guys are too insecure to be so vulnerable or even admit they have limitations. Strong men understand that transparency reveals strength. It takes strength to stay within your limitations. A strong man knows and recognizes his limitations and will not put himself in a position of failure. After all, he has nothing to prove. He *knows* he has limitations. He doesn't trust himself. He thinks, *Why would I want to put myself in a room alone with an attractive female? The odds are not good, and I am a man. I don't need nor want that kind of a challenge. The consequences could be too great. I just won't do it.* That is a strong man. I don't mean to insinuate that all attractive females are dangerous and are the problem. I am talking about over confident self-conned, bullheaded tough guys.

Whenever I counsel men who naively believe they can handle anything that comes their way, I use an illustration that, at first, doesn't seem to fit.

Daredevil Evel Knievel thought he could jump a motorcycle over Caesar's Palace in Las Vegas and make a lot of money doing it. He promoted and marketed the event until it had national coverage. He focused on the physics of the jump, the angle of attack, and what it would take to clear the palace. He was brash in his interviews and showed great toughness.

The only thing Evel didn't think about was how to land the motorcycle after he had propelled himself through the air.

On the day of the event, December 31, 1967, in front of hundreds in Las Vegas and later millions on TV, twenty-nine-year-old Evel Knievel looked really good—until the moment of impact.

His bike landed short. His hands flew off his handlebars. He tumbled forward for what seemed like hundreds of yards, his bike following his downward trajectory, hurtling end-over-end next to him.

As a result of his toughness, Knievel suffered a crushed pelvis and a crushed femur. He fractured both hips and both wrists. Both of his ankles were broken. And, of course, he had a major concussion.

Knievel hadn't counted the cost of being a tough guy who failed. If he had, I doubt he would have attempted such a dangerous jump. He had conned himself into believing his own hype.

The Looker

Tough-guy con men are in the Bible too.

Two of the most dangerous things a man can have are money and time. King David had both.

Bored one day, he walked out onto his balcony. He saw a beautiful woman bathing at her home, located just below him. David could have—and should have—turned away. But he thought, *What's the harm in looking? I can handle it.*

King David conned himself into thinking he could look upon Bathsheba and maintain self-control. This reported instance of voyeurism came after David had already convinced himself that he didn't need to go to war with his army. He could stay home and relax. And so he relaxed his eyes upon Bathsheba.

It didn't take long for David to lose control and summon Bathsheba to him. He then conned himself into believing he could sleep with her and nothing would ever come of his actions because he was in total control. But then Bathsheba got pregnant. The king's sins were surely about to be discovered.

Consequently, David devises another con to cover up his first con. He sends for Uriah, Bathsheba's husband, who had been fighting on King David's behalf—on the very battlefield David himself should have been on. David brings Uriah to his house, gets him drunk, and tries to con Uriah into sleeping with his wife so Uriah would think the baby-to-be is his. But Uriah is a man of honor—a strong man—and chooses not to lay with his wife while his brothers are on the battlefield away from their wives.

What a contrast.

Next comes the con within the con within the con. David then sends word to have Uriah sent back to the battlefield, but not just as part of the infantry. Uriah's to be placed on the front lines that he might die.

Adultery. Deception. Murder.

What a terrible and tragic series of events, and all because David thought he was invincible.

The king wasn't strong enough to stop and count the cost. After God revealed the King's secret through the prophet Nathan, David's lack of strength ultimately cost him the death of his son. If only David had stopped himself when he first saw Bathsheba.

If only he had stopped when she showed up at his doorstep.

If only he had stopped *anywhere* along the way.

But he wasn't strong enough.

He was just a tough guy conning himself more than anyone else.

The Sprinter

Now, consider another man from the Bible who was presented with the same temptation as David but acted in a totally different way.

Joseph had been sold into slavery by his brothers. With chains around his feet as a prisoner, he was put on the auction block as an animal to be sold to the highest bidder. Potiphar, essentially the chief of police in Egypt, purchased Joseph and had taken a liking to him. Potiphar brought Joseph to his own home, where Joseph served his master with humility and grace. Joseph's humble actions were rewarded, and Potiphar eventually trusted Joseph with his entire household. Consequently, Joseph had access to everything in Potiphar's house— including Potiphar's beautiful wife.

She too had taken a liking to Joseph and began her

pursuit to bed the young boy. This is how their interaction played out:

> And it came to pass after these things that his master's wife cast longing eyes on Joseph, and she said, "Lie with me." But he refused and said to his master's wife, "Look, my master does not know what is with me in the house, and he has committed all that he has to my hand. There is no one greater in this house than I, nor has he kept back anything from me but you, because you are his wife. How then can I do this great wickedness, and sin against God?" So it was, as she spoke to Joseph day by day, that he did not heed her, to lie with her or to be with her. But it happened about this time, when Joseph went into the house to do his work, and none of the men of the house was inside, that she caught him by his garment, saying, "Lie with me." But he left his garment in her hand, and fled and ran outside. (Genesis 39:7–12 NKJV)

Verse 10 tells us that not only did Joseph refuse to be with her sexually, he even refused to be around her. She came at him every day and still he said no. When she began to get forceful, he ran.

It would have been so easy for Joseph to give in. And no

one would have known. Potiphar's wife was an attractive woman, and Joseph was a young and handsome man with sexual desires himself. Their attraction seemed natural, and it would have been easy for Joseph to bed her. Then he'd have bragging rights that he'd had sex with the Chief's wife. The rest of the slaves would have been so envious. I imagine these thoughts had to have come into his mind.

But Joseph drew strength from a greater purpose. He had counted the cost, and it was far too great. Verse 9 tells us that he could not do such a wicked thing against *God*—much less his master who had entrusted him with all that was in the house.

Joseph is a great example of a strong man. We don't think a guy is strong if he walks away very often. But, sometimes, being a strong man means you have to run. To say no and walk away requires great strength. To flee temptation means being able to admit the truth about yourself.

To escape with your integrity intact means you haven't fallen for your own con.

Now, Let's Get Real

A con is designed to make you think one thing is going

on while something else entirely is happening behind the scenes. We con ourselves into thinking one thing while something else is happening. We make ourselves believe we can handle anything. Most men never set out to have an affair, but they have convinced themselves that they can handle it. This is the con while the real trap is being set to ensnare us. Strong men know their limitations and place more trust in God than they do in themselves.

When have you pushed yourself beyond a healthy boundary, believing that you were fine?

Why do we not listen to friends when they warn us of our blind spots?

How is true strength displayed when we admit our limitations?

THE CON MAN FOCUS VERSES

Ecclesiastes 10:2–3: "A wise man's heart is at his right hand, But a fool's heart at his left. Even when a fool walks along the way, He lacks wisdom, And he shows everyone that he is a fool."

Proverbs 28:26: "He who trusts in his own heart is a fool, But whoever walks wisely will be delivered."

Proverbs 12:15: "The way of a fool is right in his own eyes, But he who heeds counsel is wise."

SEVEN

THE POSER

When I was twenty years old, I had a bad case of poser-itis.

I'd work from 6 p.m. to 6 a.m., three days on and three days off. I'd come home, sleep for a few hours, then hit the gym for at least two hours. Then I'd go to the pool to get my tan on. Next, I'd jump on my motorcycle with my buddies in the early afternoon, rip off my shirt, and ride around the lake posing for the girls. If there were such a thing as selfies in that day, I would have been the selfie king, posing for anyone and everyone.

Later that night, my buddies and I would start our routine of prepping for a night out on the town. Our appearance had to be just right: starched jeans, perfect hair, everything in place. The more girls we could get to notice us, the more of a man we were. It was almost a rating system that we'd set up for ourselves, much like a body builder standing on a stage, flexing and posing for the judges. Man, did we have it all together. Or so we thought. I lived like that for two years.

I was a hurting kid who didn't know who he was. Because of my lack of a firm identity, I was willing to let the world define me. I would try anything the world had to offer to help rub dirt on my skinned-up heart.

But it became tiresome. I'd been posing for so long that it was exhausting. It seemed like the more accolades and applause I received, the more I hurt. Something had to change, and a new pair of starched jeans wasn't going to cut it.

Hiding and Burying

Posing for a photo requires you to stay as still as possible and smile your best smile. The pose is designed to give the onlooker your best shot, while you're hoping that whoever sees the photo will think you're wonderful because you're so photogenic. Today, you can also add numerous filters to your pic, enhancing your appearance beyond its sometimes brutal reality.

My family calls that "hiding the ugly." You can cover up ugly spots, rub out blemishes, shrink your fat, sparkle your eyes, and pretend to look better than you do.

Posing presents one face while hiding your true self. Posing is the opposite of being vulnerable.

Tough guys are great posers. And this poser mentality is almost instilled into us from birth. After all, most of us were taught as young boys to hold our pain in. "Shake it off, son!" "Rub some dirt on it!" "Don't you dare cry!" "Don't let them see you sweat." "Fake it 'til you make it." At the urgings of our fathers, coaches, and mentors—all of whom heard the same things from their fathers, coaches, and mentors—we learn to stuff our feelings into oblivion.

That kind of posing and toughness starts a trend. Later in life, we no longer hide scraped knees. Rather, we bury our emotional pain. No matter how much worldly dirt— sex, drugs, success, etc.—we rub on that wound, it never heals. But, just like me in my twenties, tough-guy posers keep vainly believing that's what they're supposed to do: numb the pain, bury the feelings, fake it 'til you make it.

You want the pain to go away, but you also don't want anyone to know you're hurting, so you pretend and put your "I'm fine" filter on. You don't want to show weakness, so you pose for others in hopes of their acceptance. Weakness isn't attractive, so you cover it up and stuff it away. You don't like who you are, but you're hoping that others will like you so that *you* will like you.

You play to the crowd to make yourself feel better about yourself. You pose to be seen as a tough guy.

Win the Crowd

Remember *The Gladiator*?

Maximus Meridius (Russell Crowe) was once a great general in command of Emperor Marcus Aurelius's army—until the Emperor's son, Commodus, murders his father and assumes the throne. When Maximus refuses to serve Commodus, the new emperor has Maximus's family murdered, and Maximus is arrested and forced into slavery.

Maximus's new owner, Antonius Proximo, tells him to wear a mask, to hide his true identity while fighting as a gladiator. Proximo says, "Win the crowd, and you will win your freedom."

That lie is still being peddled today. If you win the crowd and get the applause, you will finally *be* something.

But, because he doesn't want to be known, Maximus dons the mask and becomes a fearsome gladiator. His victories eventually get him back to the Colosseum, where the evil Commodus awaits. After another great victory as an enslaved gladiator, the crowd loves him. Not knowing this gladiator's true identity, Commodus then comes down from his perch to meet Maximus.

Commodus asks, "Why doesn't the hero reveal himself and tell us all your name? You do have a name?

Maximus coolly replies, "My name is Gladiator." Then he walks away, trying to maintain his pose.

Offended, Commodus says, "How dare you show your back to me." Then he shouts a name that cuts to the core of Maximus's identity. "Slave! Remove your helmet and tell me your name."

Maximus stops, takes a deep breath, and removes his helmet. Tired of posing for the crowd, weary of being someone he isn't, exhausted from denying his deep wounds of the past, Maximus turns to face the evil emperor.

With leering, vengeful eyes, Maximus reveals his true identity: "My name is Maximus Decimus Meridius, commander of the armies of the North, general of the Felix Legions, loyal servant to the true emperor, Marcus Aurelius. Father to a murdered son, husband to a murdered wife. And I will have my vengeance, in this life or the next."

The emperor is stunned into silence.

The gladiator has realized his true identity. Even more frightening for the emperor, the gladiator has chosen to live in his new identity.

Consider this: you may not like who you are because you don't *know* who you are. When you don't know who you are, you become susceptible to outside definitions. You go to work and act one way to be accepted there. You go to the gym and act another way to be accepted there. You go to church and act yet another way to be accepted there. Then you go home and try to act normal there.

How exhausting.

Who's the real you? Everyone defines you differently because you're a chameleon, adapting to the definition of your surroundings, hoping for acceptance. The problem is that the applause of the crowd can't change you.

Either you realize your birthright, as Maximus did, or you have to rely on the grace of someone who's more powerful than you.

Someone like a king.

Rechristened

In the movie *A Knight's Tale,* William Thatcher is a young boy who was given away by his father to a knight. William grows up as a servant until his knight falls over dead after a jousting match. William then seizes the opportunity to change his destiny. He takes the knight's place and pretends to be royalty.

William lives an elaborate lie but covers it up with his ability as a tough-guy jouster. His toughness garners some recognition as he begins to win jousting tournaments. Eventually, he finds himself in the championship match. Yet, on the day that his dream is within his reach, William's true identity is exposed. He's disqualified and arrested as an imposter. Not only is he thrown out of the tournament, but he's also thrown into shackles and ridiculed as a public disgrace in the town square. In just a few moments, he's gone from the heights of his dreams to the depths of his fears.

The first time I saw *A Knight's Tale,* I came out of my seat with a shout. Here's why.

How many of us are trying to be something we have no ability to be?

We don't like who we are. Or, even more terrifying, we don't know who we are. So, we try with all our might to overcome our insecurities. We work crazy hours to be seen as successful. We buy cars and houses we can't afford to be seen as high-status.

Or we turn to alcohol or drugs, medicating ourselves so we can be even better posers and pretenders. Deep down, we know we're weak, so we find ways to numb our fear of failure. We drink in hopes of being someone better than ourselves, even if just for a few hours. We take drugs to make ourselves perform better because we know we aren't up for the challenge.

In other words, we build a house of cards that can be blown down and swept away at any time. We live with the fear that our disguise could be removed and we'll be discovered as the frauds we really are. But being seen as the frauds we are—allowing ourselves to be vulnerable— is where grace begins.

NO WIMPS OR WEAKLINGS ALLOWED   117

As the townsfolk mock William, a hooded stranger approaches. When Prince Edward reveals his face, the crowd gasps. The prince admires the young lad for his talent and desire. Then something miraculous takes place.

The prince approaches William and demands that he be set free. As if that isn't enough, Prince Edward, with all the authority of the king, draws his sword and publicly knights William. Edward immediately bestows a royal heritage upon William, placing him in the royal family. With one swift act, Edward effectively changes William's last name, forever altering William's status and destiny. That's where I jumped out of my seat with a shout.

What William Thatcher hopelessly tried to do for years as a tough guy, the prince does in thirty seconds.

The False Lion

Here's the irony: Satan is a poser.

Peter wrote that "the devil walks about like a roaring lion" (1 Peter 5:8 NKJV). The most important part of that text is the word *like*. Satan *pretends* to be a roaring lion. The only thing that can stop the roar of a lion is a greater roar. Satan acts like a lion, but Jesus *is* the Lion of Judah. He isn't posing. He's the real deal.

Satan uses this world to roar at you, instilling fear and worry that you won't add up to anything. You will never be accepted or liked, so you better start flexing for your audience in hopes that they will give you a thumbs-up.

But then there is the call of the Lion of the tribe of Judah. His call is an invitation to stop posing and become who you already are: a man of great strength and courage backed by the victorious performance of Jesus. Answering this call doesn't mean doing more to be accepted by him. It means accepting what he's *already done* on your behalf. It means agreeing to what he says about you.

Another great irony is that Jesus was called a poser as he hung in agony, dying on the cross.

"And the people stood looking on. But even the rulers with them sneered, saying, 'He saved others; let Him save Himself if He is the Christ, the chosen of God.' The soldiers also mocked Him, coming and offering Him sour wine, and saying, 'If You are the King of the Jews, save Yourself.' And an inscription also was written over Him in letters of Greek, Latin, and Hebrew: THIS

IS THE KING OF THE JEWS" (Luke 23:35–38 NKJV).

Jesus was called a poser although he was the real definition of a strong man. They laughed and mocked him, labeling him as a fake. But three days later they would see their error. They would see his power—even over death—revealed.

Don't fall for the lies of the poser who pretends to be a lion. Believe the true Lion, the one who can defeat even the greatest of enemies.

Remove Your Mask

As that twenty-something young poser, I finally came to the end of myself on a Fourth of July weekend in 1983. I was lying on my bed, likely in day-old starched jeans, recounting the weekend. I thought about all the parties I'd gone to, all the clubs I'd visited, all the girls I'd met—and all the emptiness I still felt.

I rolled off my bed and hit my knees. "God, I'm tired. I'm sorry for what I've done. I ran towards the world with my pain instead of running to you. I am hurting and need help. Please forgive me. Come take control of this mess that I have made. Amen."

No fireworks exploded. No thunder rolled. No earth-shattering feelings erupted. I just got up and said, "I'm done."

Of course, I resumed my routine the next weekend. I got dressed up and hit the town with my buddies. But when I walked into that nightclub, I got physically sick to my stomach. I didn't want to be there any longer. I didn't belong there. I had no more desire to flex and pose. God had changed my desires.

I took a cab home and left my friends and my former way of life. I started walking in a different direction. I removed my mask. I stopped posing. I believed I was a warrior for my father, a child of the king.

I can't tell you how freeing it was to finally stop trying to pretend to be something I wasn't.

When are you going to take your mask off, stop performing for the applause of others, face the evil enemy, and declare your true identity?

You are a general in the Lord's army.

You are a mighty man of valor serving the greatest commander of all generations.

You are a trained warrior wearing the armor of God.

You are victorious because he has already defeated the enemy.

Yet, you are even more than a conqueror.

You are an *heir* to the throne of the King of kings.

You are a man who has a mind filled with power, love, and sound thinking.

You are no longer enslaved to fear.

You have been set free.

Now, Let's Get Real

In decades past, dealing with emotional pain as a tough guy was seldom if ever discussed, so tough guys were taught either by word or example to stuff and hide their feelings.

At a very early age, we taught ourselves—at the urgings of our fathers, coaches, and mentors—to fake it: "Shake it off, son! Rub some dirt on it! Don't you dare cry! Don't let them see you sweat. Fake it 'til you make it."

That kind of posing and toughness started a trend. Hide your emotions and give people the perception that everything is good. Act like you are good—even when it hurts. Tough guys avoid the perception and won't talk about pain. It's a sign of weakness.

But, by his strength, Jesus faced our pain and took it to the cross so we now have a way to deal with it. Are you strong enough to admit your hurts and deal with your pain?

Can you recall a time you were instructed to hide your pain as a boy?

How do men hide their pain as adults?

What are the areas of pain in your life God is asking you to face? Are you willing to acknowledge it and give it to him?

THE POSER FOCUS VERSES

Isaiah 53:4–6: "Surely He has borne our griefs And carried our sorrows; Yet we esteemed Him stricken, Smitten by God, and afflicted. But He was wounded for our transgressions, He was bruised for our iniquities; The chastisement for our peace was upon Him, And by His stripes we are healed. All we like sheep have gone astray; We have turned, every one, to his own way; And the Lord has laid on Him the iniquity of us all."

Romans 6:5–7: "For if we have been united together in the likeness of His death, certainly we also shall be in the likeness of His resurrection, knowing this, that our old man was crucified with Him, that the body of sin might be done away with, that we should no longer be slaves of sin. For he who has died has been freed from sin."

Genesis 1:27–28: "So God created man in His own image; in the image of God He created him; male and female He created them. Then God blessed them."

EIGHT

THE INTIMIDATOR

I used to enjoy intimidating people. After all, I had a badge and an Italian-made 9-millimeter 92F Beretta that held fifteen in the clip. I was six feet one and two hundred pounds of twisted steel and sex appeal—or so I thought. I was a lean mean crime-fighting machine. I wielded intimidation like a weapon so I could maintain my often unstable position, especially in the line of duty.

As soon as I had a hint that you weren't under my control and doing what I expected you to do, I was all over you like a rat on a Cheeto! I'd come down on you with great force. After all, there were many times that my life depended on it in the back alleys of Dallas.

And then there was home.

If I had a hint that my wife or kids were slipping from my controlling grasp, I'd raise my voice ever so slightly to get their attention. Not only do I have a large frame, but I've also been blessed with strong vocal cords. I can get louder than most people, and, though now I use my voice for God's glory, I've been known to use it to gain and maintain control.

When my voice didn't work to obtain or maintain control, I'd resort to more drastic methods of getting attention and taking control. During a fight when my wife Dana had had enough of me and was willing to stand her ground, I'd punch a wall or throw a chair. I was a tough guy in action to prove I was still in control—even though my actions obviously proved I was very out of control.

Moments, days, or weeks later, I'd feel remorse for my actions. I'd ask forgiveness. I'd promise my wife, my kids, myself, and God that I wouldn't act that way again. But it kept happening. That's when I really started to question why I felt the need to control my environment through intimidation.

My conversation with myself went something like this:

"Why do you get so angry, David? Why do you shout and lose your temper?"

"Because you feel like you're losing the upper hand."

"Why do you need the upper hand?"

"Because, without being on top, you may lose control."

"Why do you need to be in control?"

"Because you feel like it's up to you to keep it all together. And if you can't control your surroundings, then how can you control the outcome?"

Why do I need to control the outcome?

Because, if it's not in your favor, you could look bad—like a failure.

Know Fear

Tough guys enjoy intimidating people. It makes us feel tough and in control.

Dale Earnhardt was a famous and successful NASCAR driver. Regarded as one of the best in the history of the sport, he won seventy-six Winston Cup races, the Daytona 500 and seven NASCAR championships, tying Richard Petty for the most all time. Earnhardt's aggressive racing style earned him the nickname "The Intimidator."

Why? Because he had no problem bumping and

pushing another driver at speeds over 150 miles per hour. His reckless style sent fear into the competition because they never knew if he'd force them into a spin or push them into a wall, leaving them on the track waiting for a wrecker and maybe an ambulance. Because of their fear, other drivers would move out of his way and let him pass. Better to be in second than to be in a wreck!

Oddly enough, Earnhardt died in a seemingly mild crash during the 2001 Daytona 500. He lost control and hit a wall. NASCAR would not be the same without his #3 on the track.

Earnhardt knew how to use fear to reaffirm his tough-guy position on the track. I can't speak to whether Earnhardt took this fear-mongering into his personal life, but I just have to look back at my own life to see how often I forgot to holster my weaponizing of fear before stepping back into my house. I needed to intimidate others so I wouldn't feel intimidated.

If you've read this far, you already know that most of us tough guys operate out of a hidden fear—a fear we may not even realize exists. When you're afraid of rejection, or failure that will lead to rejection, you then fear losing control of your surroundings. If you can control your surroundings and the people around you, you falsely believe you have control over potential rejection or failure. Your ultimate goal is avoidance of what causes you pain.

For instance, if I think you're going to reject me, I'll reject you first. Through my intimidating words or actions, I'll push you out of my world so your likely rejection of me never comes. If you want to be a part of my community, you must be under my control. You must respond accordingly to my intimidation and do what I say or else face my wrath.

What a friend, huh?

Contrast Earnhardt (or younger me) with leaders like Tony Dungy, former coach of the Super Bowl-winning Indianapolis Colts. In his book, *Quiet Strength*, Dungy outlined how he led the Colts to the pinnacle of the NFL without screaming profanities or wearing a tough-guy mask.

In his first meeting with his team as their head coach, he spoke with a low, calm, but authoritative assurance. He said, "Guys, I will never raise my voice any louder than it is right now. I won't yell and scream to get you to do what is needed. I expect you to know what to do as professionals."

Dungy, an excellent coach and a Christian, had found an inner strength that motivated him to live from who he is rather than living in fear of being fired or being unable to prove his superiority over his opponents. As his team's success would ultimately reveal, Tony Dungy walked with a contagious confidence.

Security in who you are is much more attractive than constantly having to prove who you are. The tough guy has to intimidate. The strong man just has to trust in his identity.

The two men in my next story prove that to be the case as well.

No Fear

Saul was the quintessential intimidator. He was smarter than everyone around him and he let you know it. He had his own rules and regulations he enforced. Out of a need to prove himself, he'd memorized the playbook, practiced more than anyone else, held himself to a perfect diet, spoke and wrote with eloquence, and had an unmatched intellect. He had every reason to be confident in himself. Yet he still desired to prove his supremacy and demand that others do things his way.

But, as a group of new and confident young men began

to question his methods, Saul yelled, screamed, and intimidated them with threats, trying to instill fear into their young minds. He eventually went so far with his methods that, if these men wouldn't bow to his reign and admit that he was right and they were wrong, they'd be killed!

Contrast Saul with Steve, a confident young man. He was just a teenager, but he was full of faith and understood who he was. He didn't have a need to be in control, nor did he have a need to let someone control him. When confronted with Saul's beliefs, he openly and authoritatively questioned Saul's thinking. He countered their line of thinking with his own beliefs.

This was unacceptable in Saul's camp. They launched their intimidation tactics by yelling at him and screaming insults in a rage, essentially shouting, "How dare you question us! You are nothing but a child compared to us!"

Steve didn't flinch.

Then the men grabbed Steve and carried him out to the woods, demanding that he take back what he was saying.

Still, Steve stood unfazed by their threats.

The assassins threatened to kill him.

The teenager stood strong.

The men took off their coats and laid them in a pile in front of Saul. Saul nodded. The men began to beat the boy.

As blow after blow landed against Steve's face and head, he fell on his back, knowing that his life was likely coming to an end. But, instead of attempting to overcome intimidation with intimidation, or trying to take control of a situation that had gone wildly out of control, Steve used his last breath to speak words of forgiveness: "Lord, do not charge them with this sin" (Acts 7:60).

The words stopped the men in their tracks, but it was too late.

Steve shut his eyes and died.

What kind of strength was this? He was just a kid, yet they couldn't intimidate him.

As the men began to put their coats back on and walk away from yet another assassination, an air of confusion surrounded them.

Maybe they thought, *This young man had something none of us have: an assurance of who he was, where he was going, and what his purpose was. He died with no regrets and no hatred, fear, or malice toward us. How could he be so strong? Even in killing him, it felt like we lost. How could he do that?*

Saul had to have been thinking along those lines.

How could Steve had shown such strength in weakness, such resolve in the face of such intense intimidation?

Because he'd seen it demonstrated for him.

True Control

Not too long before that event, another man had shown great strength and courage.

Saul and his team had not been able to control this man, and they hated that, so they pressured the government to have him arrested on some trumped-up charges. In court, a judge asked the man, "What do you have to say for yourself?"

The man stood there in silence, bleeding from the beatings he'd already taken by corrupt police officers and officials.

Perturbed by his silence, the judge goaded him. "Don't you know I have the power to kill you or release you?"

If there were a moment to be intimidated, that was it.

But this man couldn't be intimidated.

The man finally spoke. "You have no power over me. All the power is in the hands of my Father. If He wills this, then let it be so."

The officials were enraged. They dragged him outside the town, just like young Steve. Then they nailed him to a tree and stabbed him while continuing their laughing and mocking.

But, with his remaining moments, this man looked at the "intimidating" men and said, "Father, forgive them. They don't know what they are doing."

What kind of strength would allow a man to die in forgiveness toward those who were killing him?

Of course, this man was no mere man. This man was Jesus, who could have taken full control and prevented his own suffering. But he chose to trust his Father. Jesus demonstrated a strength that could not be intimidated.

How can you intimidate someone who's totally content in who they are? How can you control someone who honestly believes their life is in God's hands?

Going a step further, if I believe that God is in control of my life, my company, and my family, and my calling is to steward what he gives me, then I don't have to be in control. If I honestly believe that he is in control and I am not, then I won't desire to intimidate others to bow down or cater to my ways.

I don't have to rely on my ability. I'm confident in his ability to make it all happen. I have a greater strength that comes from another source. I can live, move, lead, manage, and even supervise in peace knowing that he has all power.

If it doesn't work out the way I think, that's OK because the outcome is in his hands. If my wife or my kids don't act like I think they should act, it's OK because they belong to him. Now, don't get me wrong. We each have a role to play: we coach our employees, we parent our children, and we love and protect our wives. But we don't have to control everything around us.

A strong man doesn't need for people to know who he is or that he's the boss. He *knows* who he is and walks in a quiet strength, understanding that his Boss has it all under control.

If this chapter has felt like you've read more about yourself than you'd like, I challenge you to give up your role as the intimidator. Become the confident leader God wants you to be. People will follow you because they want to, not because they have to. And those kinds of followers are much more loyal and will stick with you through thick and thin. Earn their trust instead of demanding their allegiance.

Lay down your weapons of fear. Arm yourself with trust in the One who created you.

Now, Let's Get Real

Fear is always screaming at you to get it under control or risk losing. Losing may look like rejection, failure, or being discovered that you aren't as tough and secure as you led everyone to believe.

I must control to be secure. I decide who is in my world, and I must be able to control everyone in my world. So, at the very hint that you don't agree with me, or any appearance that you are against me, triggers a sense of fear that causes me to dominate the environment to make sure I'm safe.

Simply put, out of fear, I use fear to intimidate and control.

But a strong man doesn't try to intimidate to get his way. He chooses love and sacrifice to lead him. Jesus demonstrated this when he laid down his life for us and demonstrated unconditional love for us by offering a life of freedom to choose this love and what he has for us. We are then changed by his love instead of a fear of hell. Now we can lay down our intimidation tactics and relax in him.

Where does fear still reside in your life? How do you use fear to manipulate others?

How can you exchange the fear you have for the faith you need?

What areas of your life do you know that it is time to lay at the feet of Jesus regardless of how it may make you look?

THE INTIMIDATOR FOCUS VERSES

1 John 4:16: "And we have known and believed the love that God has for us. God is love, and he who abides in love abides in God, and God in him."

1 Peter 4:8: "And above all things have fervent love for one another, for "love will cover a multitude of sins."

Jeremiah 31:3: "The Lord has appeared of old to me, saying: 'Yes, I have loved you with an everlasting love; Therefore with lovingkindness I have drawn you.'"

NINE

THE AVOIDER

I s one of your close relationships suffering through a cold war?

The Cold War began in the aftermath of World War II. America and the USSR had joined forces to stop a common enemy, Nazi Germany. After the Nazis were defeated, there seemed to be a hopeful belief that the two world superpowers could get along. But their foundational ideologies—capitalism and communism— were so oppositional that any kind of lasting connection would prove impossible.

Instead, what could have been a powerful relationship for the good of the world quickly declined into a silent war for dominance. The desire to be the preeminent nation on the globe led both America and the USSR (now Russia) to seek influence and power over secondary nations. Neither side launched a physical attack on the other, but both countries quietly and constantly worked behind the scenes to gain as much control as possible.

Sound familiar?

Maybe your personal cold war is within your marriage, a friendship, or a professional relationship. What was once a strong and even thriving connection has turned into an extended silent fight.

In thirty years of marriage, Dana and I have endured multiple cold wars. We were both accomplished at this particular kind of fighting. I was raised by a father who may have been a cold war expert. He could give someone the silent treatment for months. Consequently, because it was modeled for me, I became very adept at that non-fighting fighting technique. I stowed it in my relational arsenal for future deployment in extreme circumstances.

Or just in instances where I felt wronged and needed to prove my rightness. If Dana and I were at odds or had disagreements on several issues, one of us—typically me —would give the other the silent treatment as a punish-ment. I'd ignore her and avoid her. She would know how upset I was by how long I could keep from talking to her. Oh, we were still married and sleeping in the same bed, but we might as well have been living miles apart due to our cold war.

I was so sure that my tactics would make her see my way.

But calling it the silent treatment isn't quite accurate. Depending on the nature of the battle at hand, I wouldn't stay silent about it to other people in my life. I'd complain to my buddies. Or I'd talk to my parents. Or—and I don't recommend this at all—I'd bring the kids into the argument. Just like the national super-powers who fought for control by bringing in secondary countries, I'd try to prove my worth by bringing in secondary relationships that really had nothing to do with the problem at hand. It was just my way of trying to solve the problem without addressing the real issues.

That's how I'd build my case, compile my evidence, prove my superiority, and win our personal cold war.

Guess how often that worked?

Are You an Ostrich?

Fighting a cold war in your marriage is really just

sticking your head in the sand and hoping your preferred outcome occurs without you having to change.

That phrase—bury your head in the sand—is an old myth used to describe how an ostrich supposedly protects itself from predators. If the ostrich can't see its predator, then surely the predator can't see the ostrich. We use the phrase because it's shorthand for naive avoidance. The problem is still there—and likely even more devastating—because the ostrich refuses to face the dire facts of his situation.

The truth is, ostriches aren't that dumb. They don't bury their heads in the sand to avoid detection. If that had been the case, I'm sure no ostriches would exist today. Ostriches do lower their heads to eat and hide, but they don't consciously choose to avoid confrontation by not looking at the source of their fears.

Unfortunately, we're often not as smart as the ostrich. We bury our heads in whatever sand we can find to avoid conflict we know will hurt us. Avoidance is so much easier than engagement.

I believe that's why we have such a large fatherless generation these days. A father looks at the tasks at hand —the daily responsibilities, the financial requirements, the time commitment, the relational costs—then considers himself and what he's capable of accomplish-ing. It's as if he places himself on one side of a scale and all of his fatherly responsibilities on the other side and quickly sees the gaping disparity. He believes the job is too tough for him, so he checks out, cheats on, or walks out.

I get it. I've had some of those same thoughts and tendencies at times. I've fantasized about a better life with less pressure and more fun. When I look at myself as a father and husband, at what's required of me in those roles, I see how lacking I really am. I could—and have—buckled under that pressure.

But I've chosen to no longer stick my head in the sand.

It makes it hard to hear when God is talking to you.

Are You Humble?

"God resists the proud, but gives grace to the humble" (James 4:6 NKJV).

Every tough guy should memorize that verse because it cuts against the grain of our souls. Either we were not raised to be humble or we learned to be proud by neces-sity. After all, we had a lot of insecurities to cover up with our arrogant self-confidence.

Our insecurities whisper to us, "Don't show weakness or you will be discovered for the fraud that you are." Our fears shout at us, "Strut, don't bow, or else you won't be respected." Our arrogance says, "You can handle this." But our pride says, "If you can't, you can just leave."

How do we drown out those voices? By pulling your head out of the sand—or wherever else your head may be stuck—and listening to God's voice.

The truth is, I can't be the man my wife and children need me to be. I don't have that kind of inner strength without someone else providing the power. Thank God that I'm not supposed to live this life on my own, forever alone, forever an orphan. I'm supposed to rely on a strength, wisdom, and joy I don't innately possess. Yet there's one requirement for obtaining that kind of strength: humility.

If you think you're a humble man, honestly answer this question: Do you pray out loud with your wife at night?

I'm not just asking if you pray *for* her. I'm asking if you pray with her about *your* need for help and direction. In other words, are you humble before both God and your wife on a daily basis?

Now, I'm not trying to guilt you into praying. I know a

lot of men, myself sometimes included, who struggle with consistently praying with their wives. Why is that? Because praying like that means being vulnerable. It means acknowledging what we often work so hard to cover up: we don't have all the answers. Shoot: as tough guys we don't even like to ask for directions, much less help with our life decisions. So, willingly and openly admitting to our wives that we need any kind of help is a blow to our machismo.

Here's the brutal truth you already know to be true: your wife *knows* you don't have all the answers. She already knows you need help.

And here's the irony about seeming "weak" in front of your wife as you pray for your needs: that humbling posture will elevate you in her eyes. She will think more of you when you take her by the hand and lead her in prayer, the both of you asking for strength and wisdom from God on how to lead your family.

Great power resides within the man who leads his wife in prayer. In fact, so much power exists there that it scares the devil. He will amass his forces to keep you from humbling yourself. But your General is stronger. If you want to be one of his most effective soldiers, hit your knees and start fighting back with your prayers.

When you hold your head high and you puff your chest out, you're an easy target. But when you've humbled yourself on your knees in prayer, you're an unbeatable foe. When you're united with your wife in prayer on a consistent basis, God's power can then flow through you, your wife, and your family's lives.

That's how a strong man leads.

People often ask Dana and me why we have such a great marriage. I always answer, "It's because we fight all the time." They laugh. I laugh. But it's true.

When they press for details, saying something about how they've never seen us fight, I tell them about the phrase we use when we're in an argument: We want to be face-to-face, chest-to-chest, hand-to-hand, and heart-to-heart.

In other words, when something comes between us, we fight like crazy to eradicate it. Both of us are always on alert for possible problems. We strive hard to stay on the same page. We don't avoid the issue so that it could fester into a serious situation. We "fight" early so we don't have to fight long.

And, of course, we pray for help from the only One who can really help us.

Addressing issues upfront requires more work and strength than just letting things slide. But the reward is a vibrant, thriving marriage.

When I put energy and effort into my marriage—when I focus on Dana and my kids more than myself—I love the return I receive. The results are much better and more rewarding than what I could have ever hoped to achieve by sticking my head in the sand and avoiding my family.

Are You Strong?

I can't say I fully learned the lesson about not avoiding the hard things in life until I wanted to quit my job. Few things make a tough man flex his ego more than a job where he feels underappreciated or disrespected.

For a few years, I had a very nice job as a bodyguard for a high-profile client. But I didn't like the way I was being treated. I prayed—well, I complained—to God about my job: "Lord, I'm ready. Get me out of here now!"

He replied rather bluntly: "Son, you are going to be here a little while longer."

I thought, *A little while longer? What does that mean!? I'm done! I don't have to stay here and take this kind of treatment.*

Like the patient father he is, God replied, "Stay, David. I have something here for you."

Then the wise words of my grandfather came to mind: "It's not OK to quit your job because you're frustrated, but it's OK to be frustrated because it's time to quit. Knowing the difference is very important."

I had to be patient—a character trait that seldom comes naturally to tough guys. I also had to allow myself to feel uncomfortable for reasons I wouldn't understand. My grandpa also used to say, "David, always run *toward* the tension. Deal with it." I'm ashamed to say I didn't always follow that advice, even though maybe his words are one reason I eventually took a job where I was forced to run toward tension.

Did you know that cows run away from oncoming storms, but buffalo run headlong *into* oncoming storms? Who suffers more?

If the cows are lucky, maybe they do get away from the storm every now and then. But they more often end up running *with* the storm, remaining within the wind, rain, and thunder and lightning much longer than they thought they would. In their attempt to avoid the inevitable, they make their suffering last longer.

The buffalo must be smarter. By running *toward* the storm, they intentionally expose themselves to its beating. But the length of their suffering is much less than what the cows typically endure.

So, are you a cow or a buffalo?

I had to be a buffalo for my jobs, but I was often a cow in my personal life. What tough guy wants to seek discomfort and conflict *intentionally*? Yet that's what I felt like I was asked to do by staying in that bodyguard job long after I was ready to quit. I wanted to run away like a cow from an oncoming storm, but God was asking me to brave the inevitable.

The next day I had to work following my whining to God, I experienced his strength in a new way. I realized I couldn't face another day—at my job or at my home— without God's strength working through me. Despite appearances, I was *not* a tough guy. I was a strong man because of Jesus within me. And it was only through his strength that I'd be able to endure any disrespect, frustration, or discomfort.

When his strength began to flow through me, I began to operate on an entirely new level. And, wouldn't you know it, it wasn't long before God promoted me and moved me away from that job. Had I left when I'd wanted to, I wouldn't have experienced what God had sought to teach me. During that season, he provided me with tools and ideas I still use today.

Often, God puts us in difficult situations, whether at work, at home, or in some other area of our lives, to build our character. Like the master potter he is, he wants to mold us into the image of his son, the only true strong man. When we quit in the middle of the construction, we delay what God is ultimately trying to accomplish with our lives.

You may be working in a bad environment and hating every minute. Or your marriage may be on the edge of destruction. It's easy to say, "I'm done" and walk away. Tough guys do it all the time, a sure sign that their strength is only skin-deep.

But that's not you. You have the power of Christ living, moving, and breathing within you.

Don't stick your head in the sand.

Don't quit.

Don't walk away.

My Last weekend with Bad news - wanting to stick my head in the sand

In your moments of trial, learn to rely on God's strength.

He wants to see your marriage, your job, and your life be

My wife - didn't do well either. But Ran into A friend she hadn't seen in 2½ years. She had gone through a similar citretation. Gave my wife Hope are struggles help others that are struggling

a success so that, like a proud father, he can point to you and say, "That's my boy!"

There examples of God's success

But what successes are won without hardships on the way?

Plus, your decisions aren't just about you, are they?

As an insecure tough guy, you may have bought into the lie that everything is about you. (I'm guilty of that too.) But when you can get past that navel-gazing mentality, you see that you're not the only one in the picture of your life. *When we get into Life problems, its easy to Automatically say, it is about me. If your married* Who else near you needs your strength and stead- *who does your wife look towards for help?* fastness? *If you fail in the world eyes who's faultiest?* Your wife? Your kids? Your extended family? Your friends? Your coworkers? Your boss? Your employees? Your church?

Maybe God has placed you in challenging situations so that your experiences and reliance on God can eventually help others through the same situation. If you give up before getting through, you won't be able to help the people who may need you to be a model of God's love and wisdom on earth.

Yes, that mantle of responsibility is heavy, but you're a strong man now.

Just imagine if Jesus would have said, "I'm done" before going to the cross.

When he was in the garden of Gethsemane, he could have said, "Father, I don't want the pain of the cross. I don't feel like doing this. They can all go to hell as far as I'm concerned. I'm ready to go home!"

But he didn't.

Instead, we see his emotion and his humanity as he cries through anguished drops of blood, pleading, "Father, is there any other way I can do this? If not, then I will go through it."

Jesus didn't avoid the pain.

Praise God he didn't. Now we have life and life more abundantly because Christ didn't give in. We have been set free from the bondage of sin and death, from the bondage of fear and failure, to be a blessing to others who are hurting and wounded and to show them a strength that is available to all who would believe.

Because of the ultimate Strong Man, we can all be strong men.

Now, Let's Get Real

Tough guys can give a "I couldn't care less" attitude toward something, trying to show that they are too tough to deal with such a trivial issue. Or, they decide to punish someone with the silent treatment. Both of these tactics are due to a lack of strength and an inability to deal with conflict.

It takes more strength to deal appropriately with conflict than it does to avoid the issue. As our source of strength, Jesus didn't avoid the pain of the cross or any other conflict that came his way. Through the assurance of who we are in him, we can address conflict and issues without feeling like we are at risk of losing.

Where have you used Cold-War tactics to avoid conflict?

Why is it easier to walk away than it is to work it out?

Where are the stress and challenges in your life today that you know you need to face?

Everyday — my physical pain.

my wife's expectation

my Parents

my sisters & their Husbands expectation

Doctors

The system

THE AVOIDER FOCUS VERSES

Luke 22:41–42: "And He was withdrawn from them about a stone's throw, and He knelt down and prayed, saying, 'Father, if it is Your will, take this cup away from Me; nevertheless not My will, but Yours, be done.'"

Matthew 16:21: "From that time Jesus began to show to His disciples that He must go to Jerusalem, and suffer many things from the elders and chief priests and scribes, and be killed, and be raised the third day."

Hebrews 12:14–15: "Pursue peace with all people, and holiness, without which no one will see the Lord: looking carefully lest anyone fall short of the grace of God; lest any root of bitterness springing up cause trouble, and by this many become defiled."

TEN

THE BUILDER: LEAVING A LASTING LEGACY

Next to my wife, my grandfather is the most selfless person I have ever known.

As a young man, I watched my grandfather grind up every meal for my invalid grandmother, who was afflicted with Huntington's Disease. Then he'd feed her with a liquid syringe, always very careful not to make her choke. Every feeding was a messy endeavor with a long cleanup, both in the kitchen and of my grandmother. He did this routine three times a day for a decade.

But what amazed me even more was that I always saw him do so with a smile on his face.

Huntington's causes the progressive breakdown of nerve

cells in the brain. It's an ugly, inherited disease that still has no cure. Victims lose control of their emotions, then their brain functions, and then their voluntary muscle control. Most victims die very early. Yet my grandmother lived well into her late years simply because my selfless grandfather refused to put her in a home. He felt that it was his duty—no, his honor—to care for his wife's every need.

Maybe some of that stemmed from how forgotten and uncared-for my grandfather might have felt for his entire life. He was the product of an affair that my great grandpa had had, yet he was raised by my great grandmother. I can't imagine how all of that worked out. My great-grandfather has an affair, gets a girl pregnant, and then brings the baby home to be raised by his wife? I doubt my grandfather was the favored child.

Yet, somehow, out of that situation, he grew to be a great man.

On the day of my grandmother's funeral, I assumed that her passing was a relief for my long-serving grandpa. But, as he stood beside me over the casket, his words shocked me: "Dave, this is the darkest day of my life. My reason for living has been taken from me."

His ailing wife's death wasn't a relief. It was a letdown.

I have never forgotten those words.

My grandfather stood about five-foot-five and weighed about 120 pounds soaking wet, but, in my eyes, he was a giant. He showed me firsthand what true sacrificial love was about.

He demonstrated the strength of a strong man.

Daily Decisions

When building something, you typically start from the ground up. You get the dirt ready, measure the height of the pad to build on, inspect the quality of the dirt, and assess the lay of the land. Then you dig into that dirt, prepare holes to pour concrete for the piers, lay pipes for plumbing, and then form the area that will contain the concrete. All of this must occur before any construction takes place.

Each of these tasks is designed to support the next task. Wherever the plumbing pipe is laid dictates where the sink, shower, and washing machine will go. Each decision affects the next. So, you must be careful to plan each decision and carry it out accordingly.

So many times in my life, I have carried out un-thought-through decisions thinking they would not affect me or anyone else. *I can do this or that, and no one will see or really be affected*. But that's not true. Every decision I make is part of what I am building.

If I am constantly in sin—maybe sin that I think no one knows about and I think no one is affected by—then I am building a pattern in my life that will affect me first and foremost. Then, my actions and the way I build my life will affect how I love my wife, how I raise my children, and how I build my legacy.

Too often, we focus on just the exteriors of our lives— what others see. We work hard on the brick façade to try tricking others into thinking we are good. But it won't be long before the foundation shows what has truly been built.

Living in North Texas for most of my life, I have experienced some strong weather. Storms and tornados are a part of every spring and summer. After a tornado or strong winds have come through, it's easy to see what was built on a good foundation and what wasn't.

Many houses, schools, shopping centers, and major buildings have storm shelters or storm rooms. These are the areas people will run to for shelter during a strong storm. Then there are those buildings that were quickly put up and won't sustain much wind at all. I am sure you've seen the news showing a storm coming through and blowing tin roofs off of awnings, trailer houses looking like they've been steamrolled, guard shacks demolished, and snow cone stands picked up and carried away. These types of structures aren't built to last, and no one counts on them in a storm.

I want to be someone people can count on when the storms of life show up. I want to be a safe place for my family to run to. I want a good reputation that stands the test of time. I want a legacy of strong men—like my grandfather—who lived for something beyond themselves.

But, if I truly want that, then I have to start building that legacy from the ground up. I have to build it to stand the test of time. Every decision I make today will affect my legacy.

Do You Want a Reputation or a Legacy?

A reputation is built without intentionality. It is a byproduct of who you are. Your actions create a belief or an opinion that is generally held by your peers and community. That reputation can be tarnished by your actions, habits, or character flaws. Your reputation can be good or bad. But it is created out of who you are and what you stand for. A reputation happens naturally.

In contrast, a legacy is intentional. It is planned out and purposeful. A legacy is a selfless perspective of something greater than your present life. A legacy benefits the next generation. A legacy plants and waters trees you know you will never get to sit under. It takes strength and integrity to live for a purpose greater than yourself and beyond your lifespan here on earth. Strong men, like my grandfather, leave legacies.

Everyone has a reputation; not everyone has a legacy.

Which do you want?

When I began to understand this, it changed my thinking. Without this perspective and forethought, we default to making daily decisions based on happiness. For example, I have needs and wants and desires, and it's up to me to fulfill those needs and desires. So, I will eat what makes me feel good, I will watch what my flesh wants to watch, and I will do what I want to do and buy what I want to buy. These are all decisions to make me happy. That's what the world tells us: You deserve a break today. You do you. If it feels good, do it—whatever makes you happy.

When I live that way, I am only working on me, and I will soon be gone. And, with my passing, everything I built will also be gone because it was all about me. I will have no legacy because I didn't consider what my legacy should be. I didn't plan accordingly.

Remember: a tough guy is focused on himself and what he needs and wants. But a strong man doesn't live his life in need because he needs nothing when he has Christ. In 2 Peter 1:3, the apostle Peter wrote that "By his divine power, God has given us everything we need for living a godly life."

If I have everything I need, then I can live out of an abundance and for more than just myself. Remember Satan's lie? He came into the garden of Eden and convinced Eve that she needed something else—but she was already made complete and in the image of God!

If I have everything I need, if I am complete in the life of Jesus, if Jesus lives and moves in me, and if I walk in his power, then my daily decisions can be for more than just me. My choices in life are dictated by the legacy Christ wants me to leave.

Should I watch this on the internet? Is this what I want to leave my son with? Is this part of what I want to build? Do I really want to do this? Will this decision get me closer to what I want to build or take me further away from it?

If it is something I want in my legacy, then I will enhance it. If it is something I would never want to give my children, grandchildren, or great-grandchildren, then I need to get rid of it.

The question to ask yourself is the same one I ask myself all the time: What am I building?

Legacy Is an Offering of Love

In 1966, a young, enthusiastic, ambitious lawyer in San Antonio, Texas, fought for the underdog in court on a regular basis. He loved to help people. During an afternoon dinner with a friend, their conversation turned to industry needs and what people could and could not afford.

In 1966, not many airlines were in operation. The airlines in existence marketed to the rich. Most people could not afford to fly. This young lawyer decided to make a way for common blue-collar workers to afford the scientific benefits of aerodynamics. He vowed to start an airline company that would offer ten-dollar flights in Texas.

With no planes in the air, he spent the next four years working on the idea and the company. When the major airlines got wind of what he was trying to do, they trumped up lawsuits to try to bleed him dry. But he persevered, even paying his own court costs while litigating the frivolous lawsuits the existent airlines were bringing against him. In fact, some of these lawsuits went all the way to the United States Supreme Court and Texas Supreme courts—twice.

What did he gain from that? Nothing, but he was committed to being a part of something that would benefit generations to come and go beyond himself.

On June 18, 1971, less than twenty-four hours removed from his last lawsuit decision, CEO Herb Kelleher had his first-voyage flight from Dallas to San Antonio on Southwest Airlines. For ten years, he ran the company very lean. He didn't even take a salary but continued to practice law to help fund the airline.

But, though he ran Southwest lean, he paid his employees well. He actually created the first profit-sharing company to make sure his employees were cared for beyond their employment with him. He chose to leverage company resources to pay cash for his planes so that when economic downturns hit, he wouldn't have to lay off his employees. At the time, most CEOs took salaries three times the amount of Mr. Kelleher's. But he had a vision that was far beyond immediate money in his pocket and far beyond his immediate comfort and wants.

Did it work?

Today, Southwest Airlines has a $22 billion annual income with $25 billion in assets. It owns over seven hundred Boeing airplanes, employs over fifty-seven thousand employees, and serves over 120 million customers a year. Herb Kelleher has been paid well for his vision—not from an annual income, but from shares of the company's public stock exchange, from people believing in his model and investing in it. If you want to buy this stock, just look at the New York Stock Exchange under the symbol LUV.

Yes, that's right. Love is the underlying business model.

Herb Kelleher's reward came when people bought into and believed in his love.

A Strong Man's Legacy

Jesus Christ put his own life into a legacy that would last over two thousand years beyond his brief three-year ministry on earth. But oh what a three years it was.

Jesus was intentional in how he invested. He was diligent to stay the course in what he was building. He made sure he built on a solid foundation. Every decision he made on a daily basis was in line with his legacy. His eyes were not focused on himself. From the time he stepped out of the carpenter's shed and into the light of the public, every move and every step led him closer to his ultimate sacrifice. His legacy would cost him his life. It would cost him everything he had to give, and, on that dark Friday afternoon, he died a brutal death so that his legacy could live forever.

What is his legacy? Who benefits from his sacrifice?

Hebrews 12:2 says that Jesus endured the hardship, the cross, and even death for the sole purpose of the joy set before Him. What was that joy?

You.

And me and anyone else who is willing to accept his offering of love.

We now have the opportunity to sit under the shade of his tree, the cross. We can now benefit from his sacrifice. He did it the right way and gave us an example of how a strong man builds a lasting legacy beyond himself.

Jesus is our model, the Strong Man we can be if only we'd lay down ourselves and choose to live in his strength. The apostle Paul says it better:

Therefore if there is any consolation in Christ, if any comfort of love, if any fellowship of the Spirit, if any affection and mercy, fulfill my joy by being like-minded, having the same love, being of one accord, of one mind. Let nothing be done through selfish ambition or conceit, but in lowliness of mind let each esteem others better than himself. Let each of you look out not only for his own interests, but also for the interests of others. Let this mind be in you which was also in Christ Jesus, who, being in the form of God, did not consider it robbery to be equal with God, but made Himself of no reputation, taking the form of a bondservant, and coming in the likeness of men. And being found in appearance as a man, He humbled Himself and became obedient to the point of death, even the death of the cross. Therefore God also has highly exalted Him and given Him the name which is above every name, that at the name of Jesus every knee should bow, of those in heaven, and of those on earth, and of those under the earth, and that every tongue should confess that Jesus Christ is Lord, to the glory of God the Father. (Philippians 2:1–11 NKJV)

Your Legacy Starts Now

It's my desire that you would lay down your insecurities, put away your fears, command the tough guy to die, and let the Strong Man of God begin to live inside of you. You will not regret this decision.

The Strong Man of Christ and His Spirit can bring you joy, completeness, and everything you are longing for right now. Nothing within a tough man or in this world can fulfill you or give you what you are truly longing for.

But Jesus, the true Strong Man, can.

Now, Let's Get Real

One of the best exercises my family and I have done together is to write a mission statement. I encourage you to do this as your last assignment. This will take some planning and some time. Gather everyone whom you want to be a part of this around a table, from your spouse to your children. Even your younger children can participate.

Tell them all input is important and that no comments or answers are dumb. Set the environment to be inclusive for a ten-year-old's answer to a sixty-year old's—and beyond. Below, I have listed sample questions to ask. I've also included the Vestal's mission statement to give you an example.

Write down every person's answer and begin the art of crafting your personal family mission statement. Have input and approval from each family member as you edit the statement until you can all agree that the statement reflects who you are, who you want to be, and what you will leave for the next generation.

What is important to this family?

How do people view this family?

How do we want people to view this family?

How do we want to be treated?

How do we treat others?

What does this family value?

THE BUILDER FOCUS VERSES

1 Corinthians 3:9–10: "For we are God's fellow workers. You are God's field, God's building. According to the grace of God given to me, like a skilled master builder I laid a foundation, and someone else is building upon it. Let each one take care how he builds upon it."

1 Peter 2:4–5: "Coming to Him as to a living stone, rejected indeed by men, but chosen by God and precious, you also, as living stones, are being built up a spiritual house, a holy priesthood, to offer up spiritual sacrifices acceptable to God through Jesus Christ."

Psalms 112:1–3: "Blessed is the man who fears the Lord, Who delights greatly in His commandments. His descendants will be mighty on earth; The generation of the upright will be blessed. Wealth and riches will be in his house, And his righteousness endures forever."

Proverbs 13:22: "A good man leaves an inheritance to his children's children, But the wealth of the sinner is stored up for the righteous."

Proverbs 20:7: "The righteous man walks in his integrity; His children are blessed after him."

The Vestal Family Mission Statement

We are a family that is intentional about who we are, what we believe, and how we live.

We choose to live a missional life rooted in the gospel of Jesus Christ, watered with worship, prayer, and his Word.

We partake in the God-ordained institution of marriage, where we build families that create and leave Christian legacies.

We give ourselves to relationships with imperfect people and choose to cultivate those relationships with encouragement, love, and forgiveness, knowing that we too need these for our own imperfections.

We work hard to be the best we can be through healthy and fit living, higher education, constant character, and implemented integrity.

We do not entertain words or events that are critical, judgmental, or discouraging in nature but will accept and conquer life's challenges as they come.

Though we work hard to be the best we can be, we value

and practice lighthearted fun aimed toward rest and relaxation.

We will be intentional about enjoying family time, family ties, and family vacations, knowing that even in those times Christ is at the center of who we are.

We will have a major impact in this world for God's glory by giving our time, talent, energy, and resources toward Christian causes.

ABOUT THE AUTHOR

DAVID VESTAL has more than twenty-five years of experience developing life-coaching and discipleship skills.

He is the founding pastor of Lighthouse Christian Fellowship Church and president of Daybreak Ministries. He is also the author of *Where Are You, God? His Presence in Our Pain.*

David and his wife, Dana, met in high school and have been married since 1986. They have three grown children and a beautiful chocolate lab, Maverick.

They have appeared on *Life Today* television with James and Betty Robison and Robert Morris of Gateway Church.

David has been a guest on several radio programs and continues to serve leaders and pastors through the Gateway Apostolic Church Network.